RUN to the WOODS

A Journey from Survival to Triumph

BY TED WINESTONE WITH LAURA HELPER

To Tara & Robert,

Thank you for helping me with my stay
I could never done it without your
help.

All the best

Ted Winton   4-25-20

ISBN: 978-1-942531-34-0

Cover Design: Kerri Mahoney
Layout: Patrick Alley

Captain Ted Publishing
runtothewoodsbook@gmail.com

FOREWORD

Ted Winestone has always shared memories and incidents of his childhood in Baranowicze, Poland, as well as his experiences during Hitler's occupation of Europe. It was, however, only after the 1979 renewing of friendships from the 1945 refugee camp in Bad Gastein, Austria, that he sought to provide permanent documentation of his experiences during this horrible time.

L-R: Willie Moll, Ted Winestone, Phillip Lazowski

Prior to this memoir, Ted spoke for five hours in 1996 to the USC Shoah Foundation. That interview can be found at the United States Holocaust Memorial Museum archive in Washington, D.C. and can also be seen online at:

https://www.youtube.com/watch?v=yTYFQIO7qpI

His story is included in the documentary *Lives Restarted*, available on Amazon Prime and through the Jewish Community Partners in Memphis.

He has borne witness to groups large and small, to family and to strangers.

Committing Ted's story to paper proved a daunting task, but in 2018, we were most fortunate to connect with Laura Helper who took on the task of organizing and editing Ted's recollections. She immersed herself in events that are beyond the imagination of most people, especially those who have known only today's freedoms. Laura has placed us next to Ted, so when we read his words, we hear Ted and feel him and see him talking with us. We are deeply grateful to Laura for making that happen.

—Joscelyn Winestone

INTRODUCTION

Ted Winestone, born Moshe Tuvia Weinstein, sits back in the simple office he keeps in his gracious home in Memphis, Tennessee. This room is modestly appointed, practical and comfortable. There is nothing but what is needed here. It is the room of a man who knows what is important.

Ted himself shares these qualities. Simply dressed, he is like his surroundings: unstudied, straightforward. His unlined face and robust physique belie his ninety years. His speech, articulate and direct, is enriched by a Slavic accent that suggests the distances he has traveled. Often a word from another language will visit his narrative; Ted speaks five languages in addition to English. His knowledge of European history is comprehensive; he touches easily on subjects ranging from royal lineage to politics, philosophy, religion, and economics. He is a voracious autodidact. A gifted student all of his life, he was able to earn a high school degree, a bachelor's degree in accounting and a law degree in swift succession after coming to America. He did this while working full time, helping to support his family and friends, and serving in the U.S. military. And all in a language that he learned only after coming to his new home.

After many years, he is seeing his story in print, a story that is extraordinary to everyone but its hero. The first son in a loving, extended family from a large village in Eastern Europe, he lived a life that was modestly privileged only in comparison to the sweeping poverty that pervaded Baranowicze. He lived in a place where anti-Semitism was ubiquitous and accepted, a manageable evil that simmered until it boiled over, taking his home, his family, his childhood. Assigned to work in a quarry by the Germans, the rest of his life capsized on the day he received a sharp kick and a warning to run. He escaped to the woods with a cousin, where he learned of the mass murder that included his parents and his little brother. Ted was ten years old. He spent the next two years in the woods, battling starvation, typhus, frostbite, lice, German soldiers, and the constant knowledge that his death was always just a gunshot or a fever away.

When Ted tells his story, he is characteristically understated. He focuses on his mistakes—how he couldn't boil a potato that first night, how he burned his coat sleeve, how he was too cowardly to kill himself on the day that a German soldier caught him and arbitrarily let him live. He traveled with an uncle who was not liked, who was indeed quite unlikeable. At ten Ted was a liability to others that he met in the woods—not a fighter, not a hunter, a builder, or a cook or a nurse. He was just a child.

Years later in America, one of the survivors of those years is Yoselofsky. He was there on the day that the Germans murdered all the Jews in the village and was able to escape. He has told Ted about that final day, about his last words with Ted's Aunt Rachel, about his last glimpse of Ted's parents. Yoselofsky believes that he has survived for a reason, that Hashem preserved him as part of his plan. Ted does not dispute his conviction but neither can he share it. He does not know why he was spared while his parents Rivka and David, his brother Noach, his cousins Solomon and Elijah and Manya were not. He cannot believe that it was anything but luck, that fragile blossom in a barren landscape.

But he has cherished that blossom. Ted has lived his life in service to those he has lost. In addition to his own academic and professional achievements, he is a loving father and husband. His devoted wife Joscelyn is eager for Ted's descendants to know from Ted what he went through, as well as the many acts of charity and kindness and support that have defined Ted's life. Ted is a leading member of the Memphis Jewish community. His intelligence and his tenacity have allowed him to survive, but it is his faith and his humanity that have given his survival meaning.

Holocaust survivors are not a monolith; each tale depicts a unique journey from pain and loss to a new way of life. Each survivor comes from a place where cruelty and sadism was omnipresent, where everything they knew and loved was torn away, where chance or wit or grit has for some reason let them survive, and hopefully prosper. So each survivor holds a testament to the brutish and the compassionate, to depravity and goodness, to despair and to the hope that this past will not define the future. Indeed, each life does hold the whole world.

—Tara McAdams Gordon, friend

The Lord will guard your
going out and your coming
in from now and to eternity.
~ Psalm 121

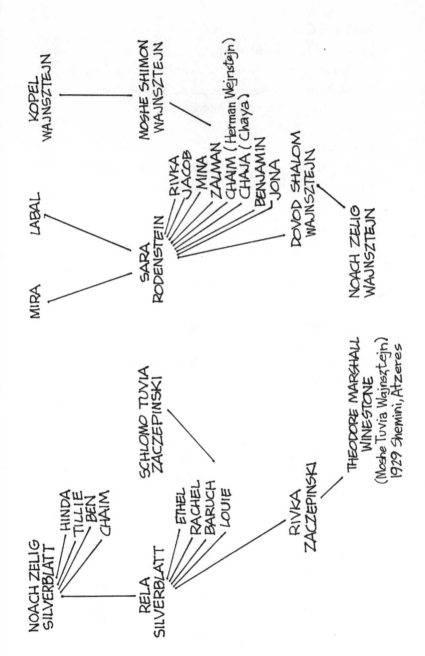

KOPEL WAJNSZTEJN

MOSHE SHIMON WAJNSZTEJN

MIRA

LABAL

SARA RODENSTEIN
- RIVKA
- JACOB
- MINA
- ZALMAN
- CHAIM (Herman Wejnsztejn)
- CHAJA (Chaya)
- BENJAMIN
- JONA

DOVOD SHALOM WAJNSZTEJN

NOACH ZELIG WAJNSZTEJN

NOACH ZELIG SILVERBLATT
- HINDA
- TILLIE
- BEN
- CHAIM

RELA SILVERBLATT
- ETHEL
- RACHEL
- BARUCH
- LOUIE

SCHLOMO TUVIA ZACZEPINSKI

RIVKA ZACZEPINSKI

THEODORE MARSHALL WINESTONE
(Moshe Tuvia Wajnsztejn)
1929 Shemini, Atzeres

11

Part I: BEFORE

1. Going back before I was born - p.15

2. 1929, Baranowicze: I'm more or less a new, 20th Century person - p. 27

3. 1939, Dereczyn: my grandmother tells me this story about this no-good son that she's got in America - p. 41

Part II: WAR

4. 1939, Baranowicze: then we were liberated by the Russians - p. 45

5. June, 1941: now the Germans were here - p.51

6. October, 1941, Dworec: a constant daily intermingling of affairs - p. 55

7. November, 1941, Dworec: when the ghetto was formed, a lot of towns around us were being liquidated already - p. 61

Part III: THE STORY OF THE WOODS

8. December 29, 1942, outside Dworec: we're on our own - p. 73

9. End of December, 1942, the Dereczyn encampment: I run into a cousin of mine - p. 79

10. End of December, 1942, the Zhetl encampment: a basement dug in the ground - p. 81

11. Early January, 1943, New Tel Aviv and Ruda Yavorska: what it was, was typhoid fever - p. 83

12. Spring 1943, New Tel Aviv: Uncle Benny's got his one goal in his mind: he's got to find his old friend Feldman - p. 87

13. Spring 1943, Nakriski: how did we live? - p. 91

14. 1943-1945, the woods: I was not much of a partisan, but... - p. 95

15. 1943 or 1944, the woods: do you see the boots on that guy? - p. 99

16. Fall 1943, the clearing in front of the swamp: a pair of shoes - p.101

17. Late fall 1943, the swamp: building the hideout - p.105

18. Winter 1943, the camp by the clearing: he gave us a pair of boots - p.109

19. January, 1944, the woods: Shlomo - p.113

20. Spring 1944, the special hideout: we lived on raw rye - p.115

21. Spring 1944, the special hideout: news - p.119

Part IV: LIBERATION

22. Spring 1944, Dereczyn: there's no Jewish part of town anymore – p.121

23. Winter 1944–45, Dworec: digging for Winestone's gold – p.125

24. Early 1945, Dereczyn: apparently you and my friend, Teddy, have a problem – p.127

25. April, 1945, to the Russian Army to Dereczyn to Poland: everything is going to be great – p.129

26. September, 1945, Lodz, Poland: cousin George Bliss with all his medals – p.133

27. September, 1945, leaving Poland: we were Greeks going home – p.137

28. September, 1945, Czechoslovakia and Austria: start speaking German or Yiddish or whatever you want to – p.141

29. October, 1945, Bad Gastein, Austria: it's a resort area! – p.143

30. Fall 1946, Italy: never in your life did you ever dream of such places – p.145

31. December, 1946, Bad Gastein, Austria: wherever they send me that's where I will go – p.147

Part V: AMERICA

32. End of January, 1947, Brooklyn: Tillie was the family – p.151

33. 1947, Brooklyn: I did what every American did – p.155

34. 1949, Memphis: they took me in like a son – p.161

Part VI: THEN AND NOW

35. December 28, 1942, Dworec: this is the day where the ghetto was liquidated – p.167

36. 1990, Dworec, the woods, Dereczyn, and Baranowicze: it was a tough trip – p.173

37. Afterthoughts: 1996, Memphis: how we did it, I don't know – p.183

Part I: BEFORE

1. Going back before I was born

My mother's family has a peculiar history. There was a rich American-Jewish planter, Max Kaplan, from Mississippi. His wife died and he went back to the old country, Poland, to get another wife. He approached a cousin of his, who had three daughters. One was my grandmother, one was Tante Hinda, one was Tante Tillie.

L-R: Tante Hinda, her brother Louis Silverblatt, Max Kaplan

The planter, Max Kaplan, wanted one of the three daughters for a wife. My great-grandfather said, "We cannot have our daughters go to America, because if they go to America they will become prostitutes." America did not have a great reputation among my people; it was only for people who *had* to go. People who were settled did not go. (My daddy's family, for example, had very few relatives who went to America.) But the rich planter said, "Look, you have three daughters and no dowries. They will remain old maids."

Finally the rich planter convinced my great-grandfather that he would do things right and the old man relented. He marched in the three daughters and said, "Which one do you want?"

L-R: Hinda, nephew Ben Pinksy (Louie's son), Moshe, Tillie Malashitsky

The planter took Hinda, he married her, and he settled with her in Drew, Mississippi as a rich planter's lady. That was my great-aunt Hinda. Aunt Tillie met and married someone from the old country and they both came over to America. I would take a guess that Tillie came over 20 years after Hinda. Her first husband died and then she remarried. She had no children.

The third sister, my great-grandfather's third daughter, was my grandmother, Rella. Her husband, my mother's father, was Shlomo Tuvia Zaczepinsky.

Noach Zelig Silverblatt (Ted's mother's mother's father)

His way of living was to go to America to work five years, saving up enough money to come back to his family and sit in the shul and study for as long as the money lasted. I don't know what kind of work he did in America. I think he was a religious functionary, since he spoke no English. Maybe a slaughterer, maybe a mohel. After his second stay in America, World War I broke out. And he went back to the old country, and sat, and learned, and went back to America. When the money ran out, back to America he went. On his final trip, he died in Connecticut.

Ted standing at maternal grandfather's grave,
Noach Zelig, in Bridgeport, Connecticut.

אבינו היקר עטרת ראשינו
הרבני מופלג ומפורסם
בתורתו ויראתו
הלך בתום ויושר עם ה׳
ואנשים
וזיכה רבים בתורתו
ללמרב תורה ה
מוה שלמה טוב׳ה
בר מישה י עקב הלוי
שהלח ג אייר תרפ״ד
ת נ צ ב ה

פינסקי

Noach Zelig Zaczepinsky (Rivka's father, Rela's husband), died 1926

I'm named after him. Tevye Pinsky. In Polish, it's *Zaczepinsky*. (I'm also named after my paternal grandfather, Moshe. Hence, Moshe Tuvia.)

My mother Rivka came from a small town, Dworec, where her family lived in the middle of the square. Going by the location of the house, and the honor that was extended to her when I came to town later, the family must have been very prominent, if not the most prominent family in town. (Her father was not from that town, but her mother was.)

My mother was not a society lady. She was more down to earth, more down with the people, because she knew everybody in town, and everybody in town knew her. She was more socially oriented, trying to

19

see what she could do for others. She made friends easily. She was involved in social work (though we didn't call it that then). There was a lot of poverty, a lot of orphans, widows. She did some match-making. Just a plain old do-gooder.

My mother was the youngest in her family. She was close to both of her sisters—Rachel and Ethel. Ethel was the older one. She probably would have been ten, fifteen years older than my mother. Rachel put on airs. Rachel dressed. But not *my* mother. But she and Rachel were devoted to one another. I mean, just you've never seen anything like it.

They lived with their grandfather. In other words, when their mother married she never moved out of the house that she grew up in. That house backs up to the Russian Orthodox church. In Dworec the "courthouse" was occupied by the Russian church; the other half was my grandfather's house—their back yard was the church. The outhouse was in a neighbor's yard. (We and our neighbors were very close. I called them my fourteenth cousins.) Across the street were some Christian Polish people and my mother was close with them. She didn't have a backyard to play in, so she played with them in theirs.

My mother had two brothers that were allowed to go to America. One settled in Ruleville, Mississippi and one settled in Bellaire, Ohio. My mother's other sister, Ethel, married the Hebrew teacher in Dworec. His name was Kominesky.

When World War I broke out, both of my mother's sisters escaped to Russia, but my mother stayed home with her mother. She spent her childhood under German occupation. She was still a little girl, and she went through the agony of a town in the midst of an uproar.

After the war, Ethel and her husband came back to Dworec. Russia became Communist, and the man that Ethel married became a Communist. But Russian Communism and his Communism did not agree. Around 1923, they moved to a big city called Vilna/Vilnius, now the capital of Lithuania.

My father's family came from a small region called Piesk. The whole area is probably a hundred square miles. Nowadays you ride in a car from place to place, it's like nothing, but when you have to walk it, it's a long ways. Their town was Dereczyn, where there were three thousand Jews.[1] (Dereczyn, that's the Polish spelling, pronounced "Derechin.") Probably about 1,500 non-Jews. It wasn't a small town—there was a lot going on.

My father's mother, Sara, was the only one I ever knew of that generation. My other grandmother and both grandfathers died before I knew them. The grandmother came from the local upper crust. The best I can figure out, and the best my recollection is, they were millers. They always had mills, flour mills. In fact, there were three mills in that particular town, Dereczyn, two of which were owned by cousins from different branches of the family. As long as a mill runs, you produce money, charge milling fees.

---

[1] They were the only Jewish family in that area who had the right to land by royal decree. It was called a "charter." They had the charter, and they also had the monopoly to produce whiskey for the entire county. That made them rich people. My father's father held himself out to be an aristocrat. But by the time it came down to us it was a historical title. By then he had just the name. He may have had learning too. The title meant nothing financially.

This was not told to me by my father. This was told to me by one of my father's brothers who visited me, visited our house, and spent three or four nights sitting around and talking about old times. It just so happened that the bedroom where I slept was right next to the room where they used to have their long conversations, and my daddy was bored stiff with all that, but nevertheless the other members of the family sat around and listened. I drilled a hole in the wall to listen to all the stories that they were sharing. Nothing to it. The walls were made out of boards nailed next to each other. In between the boards there's a little space. In order to make it livable they would paper it on both sides. You could drill through where the boards meet and there's the hole! I thought I was committing the worst crime by destroying the wall. I could not only listen to the conversation, but see the faces as they were being responded to. You could hear it better by seeing it. Now, how much credence can you give to my uncle's story? He may have been bragging, but the type of people they were backs up the story.

Rich families used to marry off their daughters depending on the amount of money they had to buy rich husbands, so the grandmother's family bought this dandy, sort of bribed him, and brought him to town to marry my grandmother. He was the bigwig for many years, until his death. He demanded their house and then he demanded the seat of honor at the schul—to sit next to the rabbi. In other words, he sat facing the congregation instead of like everybody else, facing eastward. He considered himself above everyone else. He snubbed everybody. He snubbed the rabbi. He said that the rabbi wasn't worth any particular honors, that he was more learned than the rabbi. He quit attending that particular congregation, but the pew remained, and my grandmother didn't let anyone else sit there. My grandfather had nothing but his name, but he played a big game all his life. That generated a lot of hostility in the town.

Then he died young. I guess he ate too much Jewish food. Probably a heart attack. I'm telling stories that are not only secondhand but thirdhand. He left my grandmother with teenagers and babies. They had a large family, seven sons and four daughters—11 children.

My grandmother was a widow most of her life, and a very hardy soul. She ran a tavern primarily. Jews and non-Jews came to the tavern. And she raised all the kids, most of them very outgoing people with quite forceful qualities. My father David was the favorite. He was the middle child, a slight, sickly child. His mama just loved him to the exclusion of all others. Some mothers are like that. She made no bones about it: "This is my favorite." The others resented it.

The time came for my father to go into the Russian army, and his mother said, "No, no, no, no, no, not my favorite. This beloved sickly boy, the Army's going to kill him." She says, "Here's this younger brother, who's brawny, and strong, and big, and a ne'er do well, anyway, and a troublemaker." She says to him, "You go in the Army, Chaim, tell them that your name is David, and you go to serve for him."

So Chaim goes, and he spends two, three months in the Army as David. Then he decides he doesn't need all this trouble—he ain't David. He's Chaim (Herman when he goes to America). He runs away. He comes home and his mama says, "My G-d, you're a deserter. They're going to come and kill us." So, she scrounges together a hundred rubles and she sends my uncle to America. My father was probably 18 or 19 years old, and Chaim was probably 16.

Another brother, my Uncle Benny, was very much disliked by the town. The grandfather put on airs, and Benny continued to put on airs. On top of that Benny was not the nicest guy in the world. In his own hometown, just like in his family, my father was a favorite. In fact, during World War I, he was the fire chief. They had what you might call a volunteer police department. His brother Zalman was the police chief, and he was the first one in his county to have an automobile. Couldn't drive, so he had to have a chauffeur, all the paraphernalia, the special overcoat and the eyeglasses. Very outgoing person.

But my daddy ran away from it. With the non-Jews he had a good relationship; it's with the Jews he had problems. My father didn't like the politics of his hometown. He didn't want to be part of the family that was hated by everybody, that was fighting all the time.

He moved to Dworec, where he was a Singer sewing machine salesman, which was a new kind of job. He had a horse and a wagon and sold door to door. But the Singer sewing machine thing did not work out. Then he had a liquor store, and then he ended up in the textile business.

Rivka and David Wajnsztejm

Wedding photo of Rivka and David Wajnsztejm. Top row: Jonas (law student), unknown. Middle row: landlady, Israel Iskiwitz, Rachel Iskiwitz, Ethel, Rivka, David, Manga (David's sister), Rivka's cousin, unknown, Zolmon (David's brother). Bottom row: Razel (wife of Chaim Dworecki), Sara Wajnsztejm, Rela Silberblatt, Borach Silberblatt (Rela's brother), Chaim Dworecki, Yakou Kamencki, four unknown children. Front Rug: Solar Kamencki

My parents met each other in Dworec. My father was fifteen years older than her. Somebody told me that he was in love with my mother's sister Rachel. But Rachel picked Mr. Israel Iskiwitz, and my father settled for my mother. Israel was a very wealthy man. He was a textile distributor and his house was magnificent. My daddy had some money, and with this brother-in-law's help he set up a lucrative business as a wholesale textile dealer. They used to sell the textiles to the surrounding merchants, to sell at retail.

2. 1929, Baranowicze: I'm more or less a new, 20th Century person

At birth, my name was Mosha Teva, M-O-S-H-A, Teva, T-E-V-A.

I was born on September 24, 1929, in Baranowicze, Poland. (It is now in the Republic of Belarus.) My town was a small town, 30,000 people, formed around 1900. The railroads started first and Baranowicze grew around the railroads. It was not a settled old shtetl—it was the place where all the people from the surrounding shtetls came to pursue their livelihood, because of its central location, and because of its availability to railroad transportation. The sports clubs, the general outlook of people, the commerce, the education, the social institutions: they were all 20th Century. Very robust, active, dynamic. There was no such thing as a Jewish neighborhood—even though some places were safer than others to travel in—there was just a lot of Jews living in town. So basically, I'm not a shtetl person. I'm more or less a new, 20th Century person.

We lived in four different houses, all rented. Every three or four years we would move into a bigger house.

The house that I was born in—it was in that house that my parents were married. This was the second house that my mother lived in in Baranowicze. This second house was just two rooms that we rented from a lady. She always treated me like a grandson. They had a piano. In the backyard they had a seltzer factory. They would make seltzer with a siphon. I would go to her house and bang on the piano and walk into the backyard and get a seltzer bottle and take it home. Seltzer was always on our table.

I started school in kindergarten at four years old. I went to a "tarbut," a secular Hebrew school, not a yeshiva, not a cheder. The emphasis was not on religion. In fact, religion was quite de-emphasized, though my school respected religious subjects. We took all subjects in Hebrew, except for Polish. Polish naturally had to be taught in Polish—Polish history, geography, the language itself. All the Jews, boys and girls, attended this school. It was a private school, based on tuition. If you didn't have any money, you didn't go to school, unless you went to a cheder, and there, too, the rabbi wouldn't teach you unless you paid him tuition. Most Jewish kids could not afford this school. Even some of the kids that went there couldn't afford it. Because of this I developed a dislike of private schools based on tuition. I guess my favorite subject in school would have been history, which it is today.

Maternal family at summer resort. Ted is first seated on left. Nowojelnia. Bottom row L-R: unknown, Ted, Shlomo, Noach Zelig, Chana, Elli, unknown, Chai Second row L-R: Meyer, Abraham Vworecki, David Winestone, Chana's father, Chana's mother, Sherei Shefsky, unknown. Third row L-R: Chaim Vwonecki, Rivka's aunt, Rivka, Rachel, Hadassah, Ethel Kaminesky, Yakov Kominesky, unknown, Kayla. Back row L to R: unknown, unknown

Chana (Israel's relative), Chana's mother, Rivka, Ted, Polina, Noach Zelig, David, Shlomo, Rachel, Gulia gathered at Nowojelnia

We were not a large family. Only myself and my brother, my mother and my father. My mother was a redhead but my brother and I were both dark-complected with black hair. My father also had black hair, going gray. We were not a religious family.

I think I was closer to my mother. The reason I say that, in those times if there was a problem with misbehaving there was the threat, "Wait till your daddy comes home." He would take the towel—they were linen towels—and chase after me. I wasn't about to wait for the towel.

My daddy smoked and my mother smoked, which was a rarity among women. My daddy coughed a lot and the blame was always laid on cigarettes. I remember he quit smoking a couple of times, but he couldn't make it permanent. I would steal his cigarettes. In those days people would roll their own, but my daddy had manufactured cigarettes. If things were particularly prosperous for a while they would have paper with a filter attached and you would fill this with tobacco. They called it "papa rosa." Sometimes he would splurge and have these. And I would steal these. I didn't smoke them, but I put them in the house in a little vent. Apparently he found them and that was a big infraction. I don't know why I did that. I didn't particularly care about smoking myself—I guess it was just the thing to do.

I had a brother, a younger brother Noach. I remember him being very little. They used to swaddle him, wrap him in like a diaper or a bandage. The day he was born I remember someone saying, "You have a brother," but it didn't mean anything until later on. We were never close. We tolerated each other. Probably when I played soccer he tried to join us, but he was too little. I think my brother was a good child, better behaved than I was. I had more reason to rebel.

My mother had two sons, and her rich sister also had two sons, all of us two years apart: first Shlomo, then me, then Elijah and last my brother Noach. So we had a group of four boys growing up together. My cousin Shlomo and I got along like brothers. He had more privileges than I did. He had a stamp collection, but I couldn't afford all those fancy stamps and albums. He lived in a big house. I think they tried to teach him tennis, which is for rich people. Also my family never had hot dogs but we ate them at their house, a delicacy. I always wore Shlomo's hand-me-down clothes. So I wore fancy clothes. I had a bicycle, which was a rarity. Out of a class of 50, maybe three of us had bicycles, four at the most, and I was one of them. I bought it with my own funds, my own savings.

Our background was what was called upper crust. The Jewish word was "yichas." We don't claim that nowadays, but in those days, we did, and it was a big deal. We did not consort with the lower elements. To say that we were real wealthy, no. My uncle was, but not us. We were considerably better off than the rest of the population.

We lived in a sea of dire and extreme poverty. There were many times when you could tell people were hungry, living in freezing, unheated homes. The number of orphans in the city was overwhelming. The sickness.

Israel Iskiwitz's House—Baranowicze

My rich uncle Israel and his family (Rachel, Shlomo, Elijah) lived in what seemed like a palace. They had the radio, which many of the neighbors used to congregate around at night to listen to concerts, news, what have you, under the pretext of playing chess. They had inside plumbing. People would come to look at how the inside plumbing worked. And on top of that, he had a communication center, so in case somebody in the house needed the help, needed the nanny, or needed the . . . they were very well staffed. So you rang the bell. The first ring was the room number that you were in. The second ring was who it was that you were calling.

My family lived in a small house, although it was considered very large at the time. We had two dining rooms: the main dining room, which to my memory was never used (it had very nice furniture), and then the regular dining room. Then two bedrooms. And an add-on kitchen to the house. We always had at least eight or ten people with us—not transients, but people visiting on a permanent basis. Students, relatives who were in between situations, an aunt, an older aunt who needed a home. In addition to that, we always had two maids. One supposedly was the nanny, and the other one was the housekeeper. So the house was pretty crowded, but when you don't know any better, you think it's plenty of room.

In my bedroom I had a bed and my brother had a bed. My parents had the other bedroom. The governess lived with us. We used to convert the dining room at night. We would open up the couch and that would be her room. The maid Paulina slept in the kitchen. No one would sleep in the living room but my father used to nap there. Julia was the governess, who we shared with the rich aunt and uncle Iskiwitz. The nanny, Paulina, was just for me and my brother. She was very, very devoted to us and so was I to her.

My father was part of a minyan only on holidays. We observed Shabbat, we didn't ride, we didn't work but other than that he would say the prayers at home, make a Kiddush, and then very ceremoniously would take off his cap and throw it across the room onto the hook or the couch and say, "Goodbye! I'm going to the movies." He would go by himself. We had two movie houses in town—everyone could go to the movies.

My parents didn't go out to dinner. As far as I know my mother never went to a restaurant, maybe one or two times. When we used to go to the country, there were plenty of restaurants there. Some people used to take out food from restaurants in a combination of trays packed one on top of the other with a handle. Every time my mother would see someone carrying that contraption she would say "feh!"—in Yiddish it means tasteless, ugly. It was a waste of money. If you spend 10 zlotys for a carryout meal you could use that same money and feed two families for a week.

Now my daddy was more worldly. My daddy ate in restaurants. When we would go to the country he would work in town and eat in town. And he had a lot of friends. He was just a nice guy. Several things I remember about him: he always preached not to mix with politics, not to mix into civic affairs, not to get involved in any public institutions unless you were prepared to take a beating. Business and his family, and basically that's it.

He was a little spoiled. I mean, my grandmother spoiled him, and it showed a lot in his daily behavior. Meticulous person. Never left the home unless he had his collar on straight, and the shoes had to be shined just so. The trousers pressed, always had to have a sharp crease in your pants. It was a big production—the cravat had to be just so. I remember a Friday evening when he came back from the barber shop, and he and a friend were standing on the corner, comparing who got the better haircut. They were checking their sideburns to make sure that both of them were just matched. My mother was meticulous but she didn't go in for fancy dresses.

Too much about my daddy I don't remember. I remember more about him what was told to me about him than what my own impressions were.

I later figured out that both my grandfather and my grandmother on my mother's side had sisters named "Tillie," both childless. Okay. One was in America. One was in Europe. The Aunt Tillie in America, who lived in Brooklyn, she was actually my great aunt, my maternal grandmother's sister, and she was also the sister of Tante Hinda who lived in Mississippi.

As a kid I only knew about the other Aunt Tillie, the one who was in Europe, my maternal grandfather's sister. She lived with us the last years while we were still at home. A very mean old person. She had no other choice but to live with us. She was married to a Rosh Yeshiva, the head of a religious school. When he died, she married another Rosh Yeshiva. And he died. And she peremptorily came to our city because she knew she had two wealthy nieces. The husband of one objected to living with old people in the same house. But my mother was extremely generous and she said, "You come live with us. You can be the 'balabusta,'" which means the head of the house. So she was in charge of the kitchen, the meals and the religious atmosphere of the house. I can't say anything nice about her—Tillie and I had a personal dispute going on—but she was afforded the greatest respect by my parents.

When my Aunt Tillie came, the three of us shared a room and that was one reason for the unpleasantness between us. She resented being put in the same room with two boys, but that was the only room we had. Scared the daylights out of me one time. She took off her *sheitel* (wig) and lo and behold she had white hair.

She was a religious person, very much involved in religious politics, a real know-it-all about religious matters. As kids, we felt it to be an infringement on our liberties. Every Saturday she would raise hell why we didn't go to synagogue. "You sit around with your head uncovered, and you're going to end up being an outlaw," and what have you. Apparently I had a lot of issues. I used to steal the "gribenes" (cracklings with onions) and the cakes that she would buy or bake and I would not go to schul. And I wouldn't say my prayers; I preferred playing ball on Saturday. We were just not quite the same people.

My uncle Israel was very outgoing. He was the president of the tarbut (the school), and president of some of the local banks. Very wealthy. He and my father, they got along. Not particularly close but they were in business together. I didn't like Israel when I was a kid.

He was a rich uncle and he used to have sessions in his dining room, with a great big table. You would come in. He would want to know what you had learned that week. I hated when he used to quiz me. "What'd you learn?" "Nothing!" I think he was an aspiring teacher.[2] My Aunt Rachel consorted with writers in town, and essayists, political loudmouths, that type, and had a huge home to entertain them with—a salon—old time aristocracy. Well, you become aristocracy when you have money.

Israel used to go every other year to Carlsbad in Czechoslovakia, used to attend the spas in Czechoslovakia, Austria, Germany. His wife, my Aunt Rachel, was a lady who traveled to Paris twice every year. She made several trips to Israel. The kids stayed at home, and the parent left at home would watch the business. They lived right next to the store, and there was a partner.

My people didn't go to places like that, but we did go to the country every year, spent the whole summer some fifty kilometers away in a small resort town, Nowoyelena. That was a big, social event, to spend the summer in Nowoyelena. (My mother's hometown, Dworec, was about four kilometers away.) Very thickly wooded area—supposedly that was healthy. All the relatives would converge. It was their vacation resort as well, as they couldn't afford anything else.

We rented this summer house, a cottage. We had a well. The kitchen was separate from the house. Two-hundred feet away, there's another cottage. Israel and his family had the cottage next to us. We were on a creek. You could walk across it. My daddy taught me to

[2] Another reason I didn't like Uncle Israel: in his store they had a little three-wheeled red wagon that you could carry the merchandise in. On slow days we used to go in there. One guy would push and two guys would ride. They would always chase us away because we made too much noise. Another day he caught me in the street, gave me 20 cents to buy cigarettes and when I got to the kiosk I forgot the brand he smoked. I brought back the wrong brand and he yelled at me, "How can you be so stupid!" Anyway we didn't get along. He was close with his own kids.

swim. There were places in the creek that were swimming holes. Next to the swimming hole they built what they called a plaza, which was a beach. They built dressing rooms, a dressing room for men and a dressing room for women. My mom and dad would swim together. No problem in our environment. The governess and maids did not swim. Tillie did not swim, nooo!

Next to us there was a Boy Scout summer camp. Part of their entertainment was they built a fire and ran through it. And we would go over and watch them. There was trouble—they didn't like us to watch them.

At home, we spoke French on Thursdays. That was the rule of the house, not my doing. French was supposed to have been the cosmopolitan language, and if you can speak French, you can go anyplace, and if you're anybody, you've got to know French. And in order to instill in you the ability to converse, not just to learn from a book, Thursday was devoted to French, and it was a pain in the neck. I have to admit I hated it. There was no need for it. Someone wanted to better themselves. Not only that, I called my father *Papa* and my mother *Mama*. Most of my friends used to kid me about it. They called their parents *Tateh* and *Mameh*. I was Frenchified. It separated me.

Speaking French was a quirk of my mother and her sister—I didn't know many people in town who did that. Of course, her sister really spoke French. My mother's French was not as good. I think my mother wanted to go along with her sister.

What other languages I spoke—it depended on who I spoke to or with. My parents normally, unless they would get into a funk, spoke Yiddish. Otherwise, they would require that you speak Hebrew, but that was not a Biblical Hebrew. That was the Israeli Hebrew. We did not speak German, although Yiddish is similar to German. Yiddish was the surrounding language. My nanny was

Belarussian. The maid, Paulina, and the governess, Julia, spoke Polish, so we spoke Polish with them. (The maid was not Jewish, but the governess was.) In school they taught us Polish, and we spoke Hebrew —it was compulsory. Russian and Polish have a certain affinity. They're both Slavic. If you know one you can get around in the other. English was not known, nor was it useful.

What kind of relationships did Jews have with non-Jews in the town? None. None whatsoever. The anti-Semitism was very pronounced. Of 30,000 people in Baranowicze, more than a third were Jews. Can go to theatres together, can go to restaurants together. Schools are separate. When you're little you play together.

I didn't have any non-Jewish friends, except one, and he was Belarussian. He lived in the neighborhood, and when we played ball, he would join in the ballgame. They lived probably three houses behind us, and the soccer field was right behind our house, so you just couldn't help it. You needed an eleventh person and he was a good ball player. He just played along with us. He spoke Yiddish, too. He didn't come to my house, I didn't go to his house. But then when you fight he calls you a dirty Jew. The football games between Jewish and non-Jewish teams always ended up either in a riot, or at least they were very heavily patrolled by the police department.

On certain days, even in a progressive, big city like ours, you tried not to mingle in the streets. We were always in danger, always cautious. Once, when I was eight, for some reason or other instead of going directly from my school home, I ended up on another street in a different direction. A girls' Catholic private high school also let out at the same time, and some girls chased me and surrounded me. I was in the right part of town but I didn't avoid them properly. They caught me, and I was sure that they were going to kill me. I couldn't fight back; there were too many of them. That was the worst experience I had ever had. You just didn't go into those neighborhoods. It was simple as all that. If you were caught in those neighborhoods, they would break your bones. My parents said keep out of the way.

Baranowicze had a heavier Catholic population than the other small towns, and Polish Catholic as opposed to Russian Orthodox. And the Catholics were in power, whereas the Russian church didn't count much, and they had big campaigns against us: "Don't patronize Jewish shops." Signs on the streets saying, "Jews to Palestine," "Kill the Jews" were a common occurrence. But we lived among it and didn't particularly pay much attention to it. I could ride around the city on my bike anywhere I wanted to go, but there were some places that were frightening. Some places I was very scared of, particularly close to the churches.

With non-Jewish children, there were certain things that you could never say. With Christianity, you could not say anything derogatory, because that is the ruling atmosphere. You could say something personal, something about he was blond-headed to the point of being white headed—something about being white as a goose. But nothing about religion.

Our town had two army garrisons, and so it was frequented by Polish officers. They were very anti-Semitic. On a Sunday afternoon on Main Street, you had to clear the street because they were just promenading with their ladies, and you better not be caught. No. It was not a healthy environment, at all.

I was a kid, and *Hitler* was the word for the devil that's going to come get you if you don't eat your cereal. What it meant, I didn't know. Then, as you grow older, you start reading the papers, and you notice all this aggression. First it was Czechoslovakia that went under, and then Hitler started making demands on other places, including Poland, and war was going to be imminent. Then refugees from Germany came into Poland, and they were left stranded on the border. They were neither here nor there. The stories were bad, and then you start paying attention to it. I read most of it in newspapers. The newspapers were pretty free in Poland. They had some degree of censorship, but there were many newspapers. A small town like ours had three Jewish newspapers, and I think two non-Jewish. They all went broke periodically, then another one would spring up. The rise of Nazis was obvious. I mean, even I had become aware of it, but I never realized that it was to that degree.

A wealthy relative in Memphis was sending things to us in Europe. My great aunt, my Tante Hinda, had lived with her husband in Drew, Mississippi for 20 years and they never had any children. When her husband died, she moved to Memphis, into the Gayoso Hotel, into the penthouse. A chauffeured limousine was always waiting for her downstairs. Two uniformed maids. She lived like a planter's wife. She had a lot of European relatives on her husband's side and her own side.

She was the cause of most of our people coming to the South, or coming to America in the first place. She brought a younger brother from Russia. She brought a bunch of nephews and nieces, including two uncles of mine. She brought her brother-in-law, Zaczepinsky, my grandfather, who wouldn't tolerate living in the South. There are a lot of families in the Delta to whom we are related, but we no longer claim one another.

She made a trip to her hometown in Europe in the early 1930s, and she was interviewing, and examining, and making wedding arrangements—she had a husband for this one, you know how old ladies do, and that one she will transport to America. Once a year she would bring over one immigrant to Mississippi, only one. Some of them would have to spend a year with her sister Tillie in Brooklyn to get Americanized and then get to Mississippi. That was tradition. And then she picked my mother as being the more down-to-earth person, the one with the most understanding, to be her spokesperson in Europe. The old lady used to gather up a lot of secondhand clothes, merchandise, anything, pack up big bales and ship them to our house. The express company would deliver them. Then they would open the steel clasps, unpack it. Then my mother would have a great, big sorting going on: Who gets what? Who is deserving? Who is not deserving? Then she wrote the end report of who got what, and got cussed out for doing it wrong. Every time I would visit kinfolks, I got to noticing that certain of them had things marked *Hotel Gayoso*. And I finally realized that people on my mother's side were identified by Hotel Gayoso, and if they did not have Hotel Gayoso, then they must be kinfolks on the father's side. I thought it was some kind of family emblem. I never asked or particularly cared to know more.

3. 1939, Dereczyn: my grandmother tells me this story about this no-good son that she's got in America

Now my father's brother, my Uncle Benny, liked to do everything that was not allowed. He was an outlaw for outlaw's sake. He got a truck and started running a trucking company without the license that designated where you were allowed to travel. Well, he illegally took a freight load through our town and got caught. Now the police came to our door and told my father, "Your brother is in jail and you need to come and post bond." My daddy got him out and they came home, and Benny was screaming and hollering and accused my daddy of being unfriendly to his family. In the midst of this, Benny says, "Your son has never seen his grandmother."

So they loaded me up in a truck and we drove all night—100 miles—to Dereczyn. I spent two weeks with my grandmother. She had a big home, where she maintained the grandfather's study. No one ever entered it, just like when he died in 1911. In 1939, when I visited it, the door was open and you could look into it, but no one ever entered it.

It was an active, very dynamic little city. Something was always going on. It was not a sleepy, old town. As I would walk by on the streets, most people would step aside. I couldn't figure out what all this was about. Then I realized what it was. On the first Saturday my grandmother made me go to synagogue, which is something I normally didn't do, but I'm visiting her so I have to do what she has to do. And the beadle, the shames comes to me and says, "Take me by the hand," and I'm walking right behind him, and he leads me up to the rabbi, and he sets me down in my grandfather's pew. A commotion started. No one had sat in that pew since 1911, because the grandmother maintained it, and finally, as she was getting older, she had to designate who was going to sit in the pew, and I was her favorite son's oldest son, and I was given the opportunity. Trying to give you the psychology of a small town. People were very class oriented.

One morning I got up: potatoes had to be dug up out of the ground. At a certain point in the raising of potatoes you have to cut off the flowers so that the reproduction is directed to the tubers. And that was what she was doing. She was cutting the flowers and she asked me to come to the field with her. She says she's gonna make out a will and she's gonna leave everything that she has, including her house, to my father. She went to tell me who was undeserving for this reason, this one not deserving because she married rich, this one married the wrong person.

She tells me this story about this no-good son that she's got in America, Herman, and she says, "Your rich uncle Mr. Iskiwitz is going on a trip to America to see the World's Fair, would you please ask him to look up my son, and see how he's doing?" She went in the house and she took out three New Year's greeting cards—in a matter of twenty years her son in America had sent her three greeting cards and here was his address.

And, so when I went back home, I told my Uncle Israel. He went to the World's Fair and he went to Brooklyn and he saw this uncle, Herman, who was a house painter there. Uncle Israel wrote us yes, he saw the son, and he was nothing to write home about. In the course of this visit, Israel also met Tillie, his wife's aunt (that's the American Aunt Tillie, my grandmother's sister).

And when my Uncle Israel Iskiwitz went to Memphis on that trip in 1939, he wrote to us that the Jews in Memphis were so bad off, that if it weren't for the problems that the Jewish people were feeling in Europe, living in the Memphis Pinch was the worst thing that could happen to anybody. It was very degrading.

He took a chance in going. There were words that some people believed, that there was going to be a bad time; some people said that there wasn't. Two months later the war broke out.

Part II: WAR

4. 1939, Baranowicze: then we were liberated by the Russians

The Polish-German war started in 1939. The war started September 1st. On the 13th or the 14th, during the New Year's holidays, Rosh Hashanah, I saw nine shiny birds in the sky, in formation. In the fall, you think the birds are flying south, and then I said, "Gee whiz, that's not birds." The birds were flying in the wrong direction. "That looks more like planes." I had not seen planes before. They were a beautiful sight. The next thing you know, the bombs started falling.

When the first bombs started falling on our city, we ran outside. My mother jumped and covered her body over her nephew Shlomo, and not over her own little boys, who were right next to her. Now that could have been a coincidence but they were very, very close sisters. Several houses were destroyed. They were German planes.

The next day my daddy got hold of a horse and a wagon and we loaded up and we went to a village about ten or fifteen kilometers from Baranowicze. My daddy knew some people there and they directed us to an isolated farm and house. We spent a couple of days in a barn. We felt that anything that was going to happen to us was by the Germans, but then we were liberated by the Russians. That was a surprise. So we went back home.

Poland was divided into two parts, the Russian part and the

German part. The Russians, the Red Army, came to our town on September the 17th. We were fortunate to be under the Russian part. There, again, our family was not quite the accepted part. Aunt Rachel's home was confiscated. Her business was gone. My daddy was a merchant, and all the merchants were shipped to Siberia. He thought he was lucky to escape that fate. He was smart enough to procure a union card to show that he was not really the owner, but an employee of the store, which made him sort of legal. He hid the materials—the textiles—of the store. But his business was gone. My father became a proletarian, a bookkeeper. And so now we're under the Russian domination, and for children it was pure heaven. Schools were opened up. Education was free. Healthcare was free. For children organized sports, organized activities. They did one fantastic job of indoctrinating a whole generation of kids. We were dyed-in-the-wool Communists, ready to die for Lenin, ready to die for Stalin. This was it.

Anti-Semitism was officially abolished. The freedom that the Russians offered us in those two years was absolutely unheard of. On the other hand, they destroyed religion. That first year I went to my same school, but now it was conducted in Yiddish, not in Hebrew. They prohibited the study of Hebrew, which for us was fine. It was a dead issue anyway, and we had mostly abandoned all that nonsense—just the old fogies were hanging onto it. The Russian Communists had decided that Hebrew was a counter-revolutionary language, whereas Yiddish was the language of the masses. They also taught us Russian.

In order to fight religion, they abolished the seven-day week in favor of a six-day week. So there were no Saturdays and there were no Sundays. You worked five days and you had the sixth day off. So really you had five weeks in a month. On the sixth day, on the 12th day, on the 18th day, on the 24th day, was your day off. And not everyone was on the same cycle—some had the day off on the 23rd, or on the 22nd.

But here's some concepts you don't abandon: Jewish holidays. Friday evening meals. Lighting candles. We thought of ourselves as being very, very moderate and progressive people—the fact that you light candles, what's the big deal? In fact, we heard of some Russian Bolsheviks who before did the same way. During the day they preached all this gospel about Marx and religion being the opiate of the masses, but they kept kosher at home. Kosher I kept till I was 14. My mother's home, till the very last minute, was always kosher.

We all still knew when Shabbat was—Saturday used to land at different times in the school cycle—but we still had to go to school. It didn't matter to me, as I did not observe any of the Saturday rules. My brother, on the other hand, was too stubborn. He would go to school, but he would not write on the Shabbos. He was not a shy boy. He would not violate the Sabbath—he was punished for it (nothing terrible). I never did realize why, I never figured it out. My mother and father said if he keeps up with all this nonsense we would move to Siberia, but he didn't care.

I cared, though—I didn't want to leave. I was part of the youth movement of the Communist Party. Our job was to talk Communism and go out in the next village and teach the peasants how to read and write in Russian. This was 1939, '40, and '41. They bring in about 10, 15 peasants, and we would teach them on the blackboard the letters. We didn't teach them how to speak Russian. They were born speaking it.

The first year when the Russians came to us, my father wanted me to go to cavalry school, unbelievable as that may be. I don't know why he wanted me to go there. I hated every minute of it. I never had good experiences with horses. All we got to do, the beginners, was just brush them, and clean them. The horses were not always cooperative. You had to watch out—a horse would kick you. I was glad to get away from it. After that I was in an agricultural school the first year, a lot of agricultural theory, not practice. This first year was Yiddish, no Polish.

Then in the second year I went to a Russian school. The same kids, the same place. This year is purely Russian. It wasn't easy, but it never took me much trouble to adapt to a new language. I could speak Polish, which is similar, and Belarussian, which is a mixture of Polish and Russian. I learned how to read German and to differentiate German from Yiddish.[3] Now we don't have to pay tuition. There are a few non-Jews in the school. At that time the Russians did not allow any racism—everybody was equal. But there was more competition now. I never thought I was such a good student, but I was one of the better ones. In the Russian school I was a class leader in every subject.

There was a music school and I would go three times a week. A teacher taught me how to play the violin, and I'm not a singer but I sang in a choir. Our choir was directed by a very talented Polish choirmaster who had escaped from Poland, so we were involved in a choir competition, which was unheard of. The county we won, and then we went to Belarus, which was the Republic, to Minsk. I was with a bunch of kids who were never out of town, and there we were in competitions, treated royally. We won the competition in Minsk and went to Moscow! Now, this is an unheard-of story. I was in Moscow three days. I saw the Kremlin, with the bells ringing, the whole bit. They had something that was called "Fabryczna Kuchnia," which means "Factory Kitchen." It was like a big McDonald's. It was the first time in our lives we ate hamburgers with French fries.

---

[3] Yiddish is a lot like German—it is old German, mixed with Hebrew words, together with the phrases of the common language that surrounds you. So Jews from Hungary speak a different language than the Yiddish that the Polish Jews would speak.

Meanwhile, my Aunt Rachel was transferring capital to Uncle Israel in America. She wasn't sure that she would be able to save the money here. She hoped she would be able to get to America. At that time they were going to Lithuania. There was a Japanese representative in Lithuania, and he would issue passports for people who wanted to get out of Lithuania and he would issue passports for them to go to remote islands owned by the Dutch. Once they got the passport they would get on the train and the Russians would honor the passports for them to pass all the way through from Russia to Japan. About three thousand Jews survived that way. She and her children were on the way, but in crossing the border from Russia to Lithuania, the guide double-crossed her. They all came back, and they moved in with us. Now we had nine people in the house. Shlomo and Elijah slept in our formal living room.

My mother was a housekeeper at this time. Her sister Rachel is there, and Aunt Tillie is there—a lot to manage. But we had plenty of good food. My father earned a salary, and we had money.

In the early years my mother had gained a lot of weight. When the Russians came, it was no longer fashionable to be heavy, and she lost a lot of weight. I remember the dresses that she wore—dark blue with white polka dots. A lot of people thought she was my sister. My friends would say, "Your sister called." (She was 31 or 32).

5. June 1941: now the Germans were here

In June, 1941, World War II broke out. The Russians disappeared. With an eye blink they were gone. Now the Germans were here, and that's a bigger turn around, in a different direction. One, two months before the German-Russian war broke out, we were singing in a choir. A month later there's a war going on.

When the war started in 1941, we knew how to prepare for it better because of the earlier bombing. We promptly dug the trenches in the backyard so you got some kind of a shelter.

There were several German attacks on our city. The one that I remember the best, the bombs started falling, and this bigwig from the NKVD, which was the Russian Party police, jumps in the same shelter with us, and as the bombs began to explode he starts hollering, "Shema Israel," which is an outcry Jewish people use in time of need. It means, "Hear, oh Lord, you're the only G-d." So at the last minute, when the bombs were falling, he came to confession, to say, "Please, G-d, forgive me," where in his regular daily life he was very much against people of any religious conviction.

Those attacks didn't last long—it's a scary moment, but two minutes later, it's over. The siren goes off and it's like nothing's ever happened, except people talk about whose house was hit and who got killed. And most of the people who died, I never heard of, from a strange neighborhood.

The Russians retreated, and then the Germans came. And all

hell broke loose. It was a very strange feeling. That first morning there was the German motorcycles driving by, and trucks, and they were just boozing it up in their cars. Somebody said that everybody should go to a certain place, and when we got there, there was a German officer out there with a Russian rifle ordering everybody to surrender all weapons, all radios. The reason I'm telling you about the rifle, he took his rifle and he broke it in half. Now, what significance that had, I don't know.

A couple of days later the trouble started. They started harassing people to go to work, to join work parties. We had two army camps in two parts of the city. My daddy had to go to work in some kind of military organization. His papers were worthless. If they caught you in the street they put you to work. Emphasis on bodies, not on inventory.

That was the first time in my life I was hauled off to work. I'd never worked till then. And it's the first time of my life I'd been inside an army camp. We were cleaning up barracks. I was working with friends, the very ones that we played ball with in the neighborhood. Only Jews.

There was an orchard next to our house, and next to it was a house built sitting back from the street. The Germans took that house and put up some kind of a headquarters. The soldiers in that outfit were teenagers, young Germans, 16, 17, 18. They worked for a German engineering company that became militarized. I don't know the history of it—it's called a *TOT*. They wore the brown or khaki uniform of the TOT—it was not the brown of the Gestapo. They were not quite fit for the regular army. All they were supposed to do was build bridges. We kids were cleaning their boots, helping them cook. We were not getting paid. They required us to do it.

Sixteen, seventeen-year-olds, and so we thought we were having an understanding and we tried to speak German with them.

They were very nice. We used to hang around and bum cigarettes from them. We watched them kill a cow, which I'd never in my life seen.

I said, "Gee whiz, I want to play ball with them," but they didn't let us play with them. They played with two of their own teams. One of them said that the ball went inside the boundary, and the other one said it was outside. There were no nets around it, so you couldn't tell whether it did or it didn't. They were having this discussion, and a close friend of mine, he was going to be the judge. He remembered his high school German and he says, "Drienen," which means "here inside." And the Germans beat the hell out of him. Because he testified against the other group. They almost crippled him. For life. For something like that. And that's when we realized that it was not a good thing to be chummy with them.

A couple of days later they were ordered out. Later two of those guys came back, and they said that their convoy was bombed, and everybody was killed, and just the two of them survived. We had a party. We said, "Good, serves them right for beating up this guy." But that's just a kid's story.

The Germans began to organize a ghetto, which was not in our neighborhood. It was closer to those two churches. My mother went and got her assigned room in the ghetto where we were going to move to, and it was a terrible experience, you had to abandon everything at home.

One morning on the main square in town, about 300 people were hauled in. We were kids, we were just standing outside and watching. And the German machine guns surrounded them, just about ready to shoot everyone. For some reason or other, nothing happened. They just sat there, squatted like this, a whole day, and the machine guns would go off right over their heads just shooting in random directions. Then towards nightfall, they sent everybody home. My daddy was one of those inside that square.

Then a man came from my mother's hometown and told us that everything there was quiet and peaceful. You don't have all this commotion, you don't have situations where hundreds of people are being hauled off and disappearing. My daddy said, "Even if it's a short reprieve, let's get out of here." And somehow he organized two wagons, and we packed what we had, and we moved to this small town, Dworec, my mother's hometown.

We left most of our belongings in that house in Baranowicze. I remember my commendation for my—I won the scholastic honors in 6th grade. It was a small school, it's not a big deal. That little commendation, I hid in the roof of the outhouse. (We didn't have plumbing in those days.) I took my fiddle, and I hid it in the barn, as if there was a place to hide. And the bicycle was taken away by some army people. I put a note in my bicycle to the effect that whoever finds it that that's who it belongs to.

And that was the end of my time in Baranowicze.

6. October, 1941, Dworec: a constant daily intermingling of affairs

Two days later we were in Dworec, my mother's hometown, in a brand-new environment. Everything nice and quiet. I didn't know anybody. Nobody knew me.

Now, Dworec was a typical shtetl. A small Jewish little town. It's an overgrown village is what it really was. The Jewish population of Dworec was 500. The non-Jewish population was probably another 500. The town to this day probably consists of three streets, four streets at the most, and had one shul, one Catholic church, and one Russian Orthodox church; and a town square where the market used to take place on Monday and Thursday. The roofs were still thatched roofs, made out of straw. The problem with a roof like that is, it catches fire easy, so fires were pretty common in those days.

When the Russians had been in power, the Russian army had been planning on building an airfield. And I guess you had to have a lot of rocks, so that had been a big industry in that town. People would take their wagons or their pack and gather rocks and take them to the base and sell them to the Russians.

People were very, very backwards. I was appalled at the difference. The way they lived, the way they thought, the way they behaved. For instance, people were not known by their last names. People went by their name, their ancestor's name, and probably their third-generation ancestor's name. Now, the name was not always the father's. It depended on which of your parents was the more known quantity. So here, for instance, in my mother's hometown, where her mother came from, she was known as Rivka Rellat. Rella was her mother's name. Rellat, being the "of Rella" and Rella was known as Rellat nei Alzedyeks. So when they asked me, "Whose little boy are you?" and I tried to explain to them, they would say, "Oh no, you are Rivka Rellat nei Alzedyeks." That was my identity.

My mother's good relationship with non-Jewish people, that was one of the reasons we moved to Dworec when the German-Russian war broke out. Cause my mother felt at home, she knew people.

They didn't love the Jews in that little town, but they lived together. They worked in the same places. Your garden's here, and my garden is here. They were neighbors with neighbors. A lot of Jewish people were farmers in those days, small plats, naturally. The mill was Jewish. The dairy was Jewish. There was a constant daily intermingling of affairs, whereas in Baranowicze it had been very segregated. In a big city, it was very competitive. In a smaller town they were just people living next to each other.

When we moved to Dworec from Baranowicze, we didn't move into the old house. We rented a house about two blocks away. We lived in two rooms, one room on one side of the street, one room on the other side. Each of these rooms was part of a house.

My father was smart enough to notice a peculiarity in one house, a space. There were four rooms in this house. He hired a carpenter and he built a false wall with a secret entrance from underneath. It's not a forever hideout, but at least it'd give you a chance to hide out a couple of hours, okay, in case of an emergency, until the immediate danger should pass. The false wall, to the best of my memory calculation, was about 2-and-a-half-feet wide by 12-feet long. Then behind this was the entrance that would be an entry hall which was not part of the house. Right near the well, to get out to drink. He hired a local man to build it. I guess he trusted him. And then boarding up the front windows was ordered by the Germans. So we couldn't see across the street.

My daddy, being a very practical person, and having gone through the practicalities and the experiences of World War I, realized that this was going to be a repeat performance, and he buried a lot of his goods in the ground, textiles, other things. In one place he buried a lot of gold.

So the first day, we had breakfast in one house, and then I walked across to where my part of the family slept. The lady from whom we rented the room said, "Come here, little boy," and I went there, and she said, "Did you have breakfast yet?" And I said, "Yeah." She says, "What did you eat?" "I don't know." I really didn't. I was not cognizant of food. Food was something that mama made you do; if there wasn't any food it would have been all right, too. She says, "What do you mean you don't know? Did you have bread?" And I said, "I suppose so." She says, "Was it white bread or black bread?" I don't know. And then I said, "Black bread." She said, "Did you have butter with it?" All these specific questions, and I was never aware of things like that. Very uncomfortable. And she says, "Did your mother tell you not to tell?" I said, "Oh no, my mother didn't tell me anything like that." So we go to lunch. I'm sitting at my mother's table, and now I'm observing. I ask, "This is cream?" "Yeah, that's cream, and that's sour cream." Now, I'm learning, sour cream as opposed to regular cream, yeah? And this is black bread? Yes.

My mother said, "Why are you asking all these questions?" She right away figured out what was happening, because she came from that background. She said, "Number one, it's not polite to talk about food—what you eat, or what you don't eat. Food is only a sustenance. But another part is, we've got food on our table, there's always a chance that they don't. Okay? So that sets you apart. Jealousy provokes as much anger as murder. People will sometimes kill you for food. People will be envious of the fact that you're eating better than they do, and consequently they will hate you. Then there's an old Jewish thing called the 'kina hora,' that's the evil eye, they'll give you the evil eye. That's even worse than anything else," she says. "The best thing to do is play it down. If we got the cream, just enjoy the cream, and forget about it. If we had butter on the table, enjoy it, but you don't have to tell people about it." That was my first day's learning experience.

Second day's learning experience was: Potatoes. We went out to a creek behind the house where there was a pasture, and this was already the Fall of the year. And potatoes are being dug, and it's customary by the shepherds to bake the new potatoes in the ashes of a fire that they built—very tasty. I went out and I did that and I said, "My G-d, this is really the way to live." My first experience in the country.

Fall was quickly disappearing. The Jewish holidays came, there were still no Germans in town. There was just a local militia that was making the Jewish people go out and build the road between Nowoyelena, the summer resort, and Dworec. Other than that, there was no problems. The poverty was naturally great, because there were no jobs. You tried to hire yourself out as a laborer in the Fall, to thresh the wheat, dig potatoes. Those who had skills like tailors and shoemakers went out in the villages to get jobs.

The Russian priest came to call. This is World War II already, and a Jewish family moving into town is not a novelty. However, when the Russian priest came in, it scared the daylights out of me. There he was, this great, big personage, with a long black beard and a great big cross—I mean, that cross must have been five feet long, and a great big bishop's cap that he wore. Their house and the church shared the town square, and that's why probably he knew my mother. He came to call and they drank tea, and he promised to help us. But he never did.

7. November, 1941, Dworec: When the ghetto was formed, a lot of towns around us were being liquidated already

Then the German government said that you had to give up anything that had copper in it. You had to give up any furs—all warm clothes was confiscated. They said they needed it for the front for the German army. Any warm boots, shoes, coats, all that was taken away. Copper, I said, silver, gold, obviously. There was a lady in Israel who told me many years later that she was in the next town, and my daddy was one of those who transported all the wealth, so to speak, to that town. He saw her, and he said, "This is the last time we're going to see each other. It does not look good." He had a premonition that it wasn't going to work out.

Then Mr. Schindler came to our town. He's from the same organization as the famous guy, but that was not his name—the timing is not right. I'm just calling him Schindler for convenience. He had one more German with him, a chauffeur, or his attendant. We hardly ever saw any strange Germans except this Mr. "Schindler," who used to ride by with his girlfriend on his horse, and hand out orders and then that was the end of it.

Mr. Schindler's was making a ghetto. One side of the street was within the ghetto, the other side was outside the ghetto, and the barb wire goes from one house to the next one. The houses are close together, so the front yard is being barbwired. The windows are boarded up. Our house, all those houses in Poland have porches. The porches were torn off, and everybody's now moved from the rest of the town inside the ghetto.

When the ghetto was formed my family all moved to the one room on the ghetto side of the street. We were now reduced to one room in that house. We built bunks, two, three high. Sanitation facilities were nonexistent. They dug one great big old trench and that was supposed to be the outhouse.

A lot of towns around us were being liquidated already. We had a lot of refugees from those towns, people who managed to escape, among them several of my friends that I had made. The Germans made them dig a great big mass grave, and then they would bring out a bunch of people, make them undress, and then the machine guns used to cut them down, and the next group used to throw them in the grave. And then they had to undress, and go through that process themselves.

I must tell the story about a boy from the next town. He somehow fell in that grave, but he wasn't killed. He heard a German saying that he's going to take a break. He says he is tired of this heavy work of constantly having to kill. So he was taking time out, and the kid got out of the grave. He crawled out, and he went right by that German machine gunner. The gunner saw him. But that was his time out, he wasn't doing anything then. And he let him get away. The kid went home, realized that everybody was dead, so he came to our little town where he had an aunt. And then he spent the rest of the year with us. He was my age.

Another boy came to us with just as gory a story, maybe even worse. I knew him from Baranowicze. We went to the same school together. And he left Baranowicze when we did. He went with his family to a town called Haradok. They killed everyone in that town, and he came to Dworec. Of course, Mother took him in—naturally he was alone, he was orphaned by then. After spending a month in Dworec, when the wintertime came, he disappeared. Then he showed up about four months later. He had been with the partisans, and things got really bad in the woods. He brought me a bullet, a rifle bullet, a memento. And I was fool enough to carry that bullet with me—you know, if the Germans ever searched me, they would have shot me for it. But what's the purpose of a bullet? That's a kid trying to be daring. He told me all about life in the woods, which was an unbelievable story. Then he disappeared again. Wasn't but a couple of weeks later, he came back again, but this time he had a bullet in his head. They had shot him. The Germans came to the woods and circled their encampment and shot everybody. A bullet was lodged someplace in his brain. He could still move, but he couldn't talk any more. Dworec had a makeshift hospital with medical professionals, but no supplies. No medicine, nothing. I guess bandages. It was not a hospital, it was just a place for people to receive acts of mercy and to die. He stayed in that hospital a couple more weeks. And he died.

There's also a story about a cousin of mine, Manya, a girl about a year younger than myself, who showed up on our doorstep. She was about 10, 11, my father's sister's daughter. Their last name was Landau, I think. She had lived in Dereczyn, too. Their story is different. Manya had been in the woods all that summer, all that fall, until wintertime came. She was with my Uncle Benny (her uncle, too—he was my father's brother) and two other children.[4] She was in two different camps that were well organized: one made up of people from a town called Zhetl and one from Dereczyn. The Dereczyn group was near a town, and the name of the town was Ruda Yavorska.

---

[4] In their town (I may not tell it right, shouldn't tell it), Uncle Benny fell in love with a pretty woman whose father was a rabbi without a congregation. In order to be able to marry her, he organized a meeting—he had all his brothers with him—where the local rabbi was deposed and he brought in his future father-in-law and replaced the rabbi. That's why he was hated. The new rabbi was a tall redheaded man. He had very pretty looking children.

Uncle Benny's wife's sister had started consorting with a German gendarme when the Germans came. And that gendarme apparently told them that tomorrow everybody's going to be killed except for her and her family. Uncle Benny did not take a chance. He went up to the attic of the slaughterhouse in that town, and he took with him his two children, Marvin and Florence, also Manya. He also had my cousin George Bliss (his Hebrew name is Yosef; in Polish, his last name was Bliznianski) and his brothers Meshel and Siome, my daddy's sister's sons.

When the Germans came to kill everybody, either someone notified them that there were Jews hiding in the slaughterhouse or the dog gave them away but they came to get them. Benny threw the children out the window and then jumped out. He was shot—he got a bullet right in the sole of his foot—and then they all escaped to the woods, beginning with June, July of '42. Their story is that when they escaped there were several hundred of them. And then the Germans came and attacked them, killed about three-fourths of them, in the woods.

On top of that Manya contracted typhoid fever in the woods, and she was eaten up with lice. And she got a disease going around in the woods called *krudtz*, where there are boils on your skin and wounds turn up throughout your body. Manya couldn't take it. Benny wasn't particularly nice to her. (This girl was a spoiled little brat to begin with, and hated Uncle Benny from day one.) So when she found out that she had another uncle in Dworec, she ran away. She went to villages and asked how to get back to Dworec. She left the woods and came to us.

She was very ill. She showed up frostbitten, too. Of course, my mother took care of her. I happened to be in the room when she arrived and I listened. I heard her tell her story and I heard her tell names of places where partisans lived. That's how I learned those names. And I listened to her stories—where she was, where the woods were, how life was in the woods, how Uncle Benny survived what is called the *oblava*. Now, what is an oblava? An oblava is when the German Army comes like a search party and attacks whoever's in the woods. A massacre. These people were not prepared for life in the woods, and she gives me all this information, which I store in my head.

I was assigned to a group of teenagers, kids really, to go to work on the rockpile. (My father did not work on the rockpile. He worked in the local sawmill.) The Russians had left acres and acres and acres of rocks stockpiled from their work on the airfield. Now Mr. Schindler says he needs those rocks someplace else. We were to pass as a special work brigade at the end of the line where the rocks were being hauled from. There were probably 50 or 60 of us in it, and we had one supervisor. We thought we were going to be saved, because we were necessary for the German war effort. That's what he led us to believe.

The Germans hauled in mining cars on a little narrow gauge track, and we would load up the mining car with rocks and they would take them to the railroad. It was about a two-mile run. And who gets to push those little carts? The kids. You push it up the hill, and then you get to ride downhill, and then that was all the fun in the world, that was the joy of life that you looked forward to. We had to cross this little creek. The Germans made us destroy a cemetery— the cemetery next to town that had the Jewish monuments—and so we built a bridge across the creek out of the monuments. We were hungry, but we had a lot of fun in a stealthy sort of a way. Nearby, we also used the rocks to build a bridge for small railroad cars.

We used to get out in the mornings, seven days a week. In the summertime, we worked as many as 14, 16 hours a day. We tried to show off, and we outperformed the other groups. We worked on the creek, we got to swim. But work on that detail was rough. The work was very hard. Hands were calloused, cut up all the time. Because working with rocks is pretty hard. But it made you develop. It gave you physical strength. In the wintertime you were not given any gloves, and handling icy things with your bare hands can get really bad. We were kids. We tried to make the best of it.

When you marched back home at the end of the day, you tried to take a chance and bring in firewood, so at least the house would be warm. This one would bring in a piece of wood and then you create a fire. Of course, if they caught you carrying firewood, you were shot. A lot of people lived in barns, not even houses, that were converted into barracks, and they strictly froze to death.

The last time I smoked was when I worked on the rockpile. As the locomotive came to pick up the loaded wagons, the engineer on the locomotives sold tobacco and I remember buying some and giving it to my daddy and he thanked me for it, grateful as he could be. He says, "You're stealing cigarettes. You see what it is doing to me. But if you want to smoke, then smoke." And from that time I quit. Once I got permission I guess there wasn't anything to it.

"Schindler" kept bringing in Jews. When it was all over with, he had 2,500 people in that little place. The living conditions became very bad. The Germans never, not even one ounce of bread, was supplied by them. Schindler fed us nothing. I mean, he didn't care about it—y'all do the best you can. And you're not allowed to go outside to get food.

Hunger was the main thing. A Polish, non-Jewish friend of my mother used to bring us food—this was her childhood friend who grew up across street from her. They had a very close relationship. Many a time she would bring us bottles of milk, look when the guard was not looking, slip it under the wire. Very risky for her. Would risk her life. And she introduced us to people that would sell us food.

Then my mother got involved with feeding the people. We had gold. For a 10-ruble gold piece, which was like a 10-dollar piece, you can buy a whole wagon full of flour. She had connections in town, and she got that under the barbed wire, brought it into the ghetto. And they would bake bread in several ovens all night long, and in the morning they would distribute it. She became the town feeder, and so my daddy was made more or less the supervisor of the camp. I don't think there was a person other than my mother that provided the bread for the town. She was one who gives to others easily.

Even with my mother's largesse, the best you got was one slice of bread and that was to keep you all day long. People used to literally risk their lives, skip out of the camp—it was not well guarded—and go to the neighboring villages to beg, steal, borrow, do whatever they could to just beg a meal. And if they were caught, they were shot and there were many instances like that. People were just starving to death.

I carried a piece of bread in my pocket, and every once a while I would pinch off a piece and put it in my mouth, and some kids saw me do it. And they said, "Ah-ha, Winestone is in charge of the bread distribution on the base, so his kids stole the bread, and he has it, and we don't." I came home crying. I said, "They accused me of being a thief." My daddy said, "That's the way it's going to be. If you're going to be in the public eye, you're going to take abuses. They'll always accuse you of everything under the sun." I didn't steal anything—it was our bread to begin with. My mother bought it, paid for it, baked it, and distributed it.

We worked very hard, no pay, no food. Whatever quarters you

had, you had, and it was strictly patrolled and supervised by a small group of local militia, self-organized. We were hoping that that would be our mode to survival. Life in the camp was unbearable. People committed suicide. The death rate, bodies were being carried out on a daily basis to be buried outside the camp. And then when we destroyed the cemetery, they were being buried within the camp. Right there where you lived, the body was buried next to your house.

One night the Germans marched everybody out on the Dworec town square, and they kept us there all night long. We were sure we were going to die.

The advantage that I had over everybody else was that one of the supervisors was married to my mother's childhood girlfriend, the lady who gave us food. He was a Polish engineer, and he was the supervisor on the labor gang. He yanked me out from that rockpile brigade towards the end, and he gave me the job of being his clerk, his lackey, his gofer. He had a little booth, and my job was to keep the booth clean and to record how many little wagons were coming and how many were leaving. We were the first shift, our little group, particularly me, to get things ready for the day's work.

Once I went to get a shovel or something, and this German ran in the booth. He wasn't supposed to be there, but he just suddenly appeared, and he had this great big whip. He was swinging left and right. Anybody in his way was catching the whip. And I caught the tail end of that whip, and believe me, it hurt for months afterwards. There were several attacks like that by marauding Germans. Sometimes they would kill a couple of people for whatever reason, but you always thought it was someone else, it was not you—that just as long as you behaved and did your job, everything was fine.

I was an exception, I had it a lot better than others, but the misery that the others went through was just unbelievable. A group of Ukrainian soldiers were on a train; the train stopped, and the soldiers got out—they never shot at anybody, but they beat the daylights out of every one of the workers on the rockpile. I mean they maimed them. You were at everybody's mercy.

One morning, about three weeks after Manya had showed up, I went to work. Tillie was sitting in the house. She didn't give me a friendly goodbye. After working a couple of hours, the word came: the camp was surrounded by the SS people. Then the word came that everybody better get back to camp. For some reason, I did what I always did. I had to clean up the supervisor's booth and get ready for the next day, and so I did that. After cleaning it up, I walked out of the booth, and there was a couple of more stragglers—two here, three there, for whatever reason, they missed the word, and they didn't get back and they're looking to me. To be exact, there were a total of 10 of us. I'm the man who's the connection to the supervisor, what should they do? They are afraid to go by themselves, unsupervised, back to camp.

I go to the supervisor, the Polish engineer married to my mother's childhood friend, and asked him what should I do, what do we do? And he says to me, very calmly, in Polish, "Run to the woods."

I go back to my people and they say, "What did he say?" and I say, "Run to the woods." They say to me, "What does it mean?"

I go back to the booth, and I ask my supervisor again, "What does it mean, 'run to the woods?'" And he kicks me in the butt real hard. Cause I asked for the second time. I think he threw me out flying, he kicked me that hard. He said, "I told you, run to the woods."

So I go back to the people and say, "You see what he did? He just kicked me, and he said, 'run to the woods.'" And so they say, "Well, what do we do?" I said, "Well, 'run to the woods' means exactly that. Over there, there's a little wooded area, so come on, let's go to the woods." So we go on to this little wooded area on the strip.

Okay. I'm now outside the shed. My supervisor kicked me out. People surround me, are looking to me for answers. I have no answers to give them. I'm the young kid. But they're looking to me for guidance, because I am who I am—I am the son of Mr. Winestone and also the clerk of the supervisor, so I'm supposed to take them to the woods. Now we got to the woods and now what?

We're standing around and standing around and finally decide we'd better go back to town and see what's going on. But instead of all of us going, they send me and another kid a little older than me to be the scouts. There was a little creek between where we were and the labor camp. We were about 200 feet away. We came just a bit closer to reconnoiter to see what was going on. It was very quiet in the early afternoon. We're contemplating whether to go back inside or to tell our people that everything is quiet and we can go back. We just really don't know what to do, and then suddenly a mob appears from nowhere and storms the barbed wire, a mass of people just appeared from inside the camp and threw themselves bodily on one of the barbed wire fences. Jews trying to break out. And the Germans start shooting. The shooting starts. We think the shooting is for our benefit because maybe the Germans spotted us. We run away. We come back to the wooded area, we tell them the story.

Now what? We don't know what to do.

We really didn't know what had happened. We didn't hear any shooting other than that particular outburst. We spent the rest of the day in those woods, just standing. We got to be on the move. We can't be in one place. Maybe people noticed us. Don't know which way to go. We start moving. The night is pitch dark and we run into another group.

I run into, smack face-to-face, a cousin of mine, the son of my rich Uncle Israel. Shlomo was at least a head taller and stronger than me. He worked in the sawmill in the labor camp, and he and about 14 or 17 people had the same experience we did: They got away, and they're still looking to us for leadership. His group to him.

But now it's not groups. Now we're 20-some people together, we're one big group. We got up the courage and went to one peasant house. Some parts of the countryside was not all congregated in villages. They were all spread out, a house here, a house there. Each man lived on his own acreage instead of living in the village. (The cottages were called *chutar* and were for agricultural diversification.) So we go to the man who lives there and he says, "Yeah, I'll tell you what's happened in town. They killed everybody."

I broke his window. I don't know why. It's twice in my life I've done it. I broke his window and I grabbed a sack with about 5 or 10 pounds of green peas and he told us to leave, and we left and I was eating those peas for the next two, three days.

And so my town was gone, and I did not know the fate of my parents, and my history is another chapter.

Now it starts: the story of the woods.

Part III: THE STORY OF THE WOODS

8. December 29, 1942, outside Dworec: we're on our own

Now we know that there's no return. We're on our own. We are in a wooded area. I don't even know how to get to the place that Manya had described, where Uncle Benny and my cousin George Bliss are.

So the group is now 60-some strong, all kinds of stragglers together. We build a fire, we go out to get some food, but we know that this area of the woods is not thick enough for survival. There's a few acres at a stretch.

The word is that we've got to go east. Why east? East there is a known wilderness, Nalibutzka wilderness, named after the town of Nalibulke. And east is where the front is. Maybe we'll get closer to where Russia is, which is a dream in itself. But in order to go east you've got to cross the railroad, and in order to cross the railroad you got to break up into small groups, because the railroad is very heavily patrolled by German troops. So the 60 people break up. Four go away, five go away. Two go away. They're all going off in their own little groups and my cousin Shlomo is begging other people "Can we go with you?" and nobody wants us. We're kids.

I began to realize that I was just a liability. First of all I was not strong. I was not sickly, but I was not considered a strong child. I was little and I was young, inexperienced in daily life. Nobody thought I was bright.

Now we're down to 10 survivors in my group. Shlomo, his pride or whatever it was, he didn't want to be the very last one. He comes up to me and he says, "Where are they going?" and I said, "They're all going east." "Just for that," he says, "we're going west. Come on." I say, "Why west?" He says, "They don't know where they're going just like we don't know where we're going." Really the main reason we went west was they rejected us. But another reason was that I knew the village that I wanted to go to: the name of the place that was etched in my mind from my cousin Manya's stories was Ruda Yavorska.

So he and I start going west and a third person tacks on to us. Later I realized that he had epilepsy. Odd little critter, older man with epilepsy. Probably in his forties. But he knows me by name. He's going where I'm going. He's banking on me, and we start marching. We look at the moon, we figure out west, and we're going west.

Now my cousin starts a conversation with me. He says, "I think you know where you're going." I says, "I don't know where I'm going." He says, "Your cousin" (she was a cousin on the other side, Manya) "has talked to you a lot. She told you a lot of stories. What did she tell you?" and I tell him, "My Uncle Benny's in the woods. He was there two weeks ago or three weeks ago." He said, "What's the name of the place?" and I give him the name of the place: Ruda Yavorska. "Okay."

We go into the nearest house that we find. I knock on the door and I ask him, "Which is the way to Ruda Yavorska?" We ask for some bread too, and they give us bread and directions.

So we go. We have directions and we're going. We're going all night long. We go all day long. First night we stopped in a village. We asked a man to let us in his house to sleep. He wouldn't do it, so we went in the barn, plenty of straw, and we just lie down, but we remembered one thing. You got to wake up every 20 minutes to walk around so you don't freeze to death. If you lie still, the frost will get you.

Two days later we get to Ruda, and I look around. Ruda is way out in open country. Ain't no woods for miles. You can't see any, and I said, "The girl gave me wrong information. Why would she do that?" I knew she had gripes, but why would she misinform me? But I go from house to house and keep asking for partisans. People chase you away because they think you're a spy. Finally I came to realize that we made a mistake or somehow we misunderstood each other. Instead of directing us over to Ruda Yavorska, the lady directed us towards a village called Ruda, without the Yavorska. It's just like Memphis and West Memphis, okay?

We're 35 miles away from where we want to be, walking distance. So we start heading in that direction. Took us two more days, and we are now approaching Ruda Yavorska. It's nighttime. It's dark, and we're on a main highway. We're not walking the fields. My cousin's in front of me and he says, "There's somebody ahead of us." So we stop and look around. I say, "Oh, you don't know what you're talking about. There's nobody here," and I walk up front and keep walking. I know now that I was nearsighted, but I didn't know it at the time. He stops me again. He says, "There's somebody ahead of us," and I stop and I don't see nothing, I don't hear nothing and I start walking again. And then the shooting starts.

They were not Germans—they were partisans. But Shlomo went left and I went right and that's when we separated. My cousin's gone. This is when he and I separated forever. I mean, we still saw each other, but we were no longer a unit. The epileptic is still with me (though he later died in the woods). We ran off the road. There was a swamp but it was frozen over, and we hid in between the stumps over there for the night. We saw the armed people walk by.

In the morning we got up, we marched back.

Now it's beginning to snow, and we're now on the edges of the village Ruda Yavorska, and there are Germans in Ruda Yavorska. Then we came to find out that the Germans had left, but no matter who I ask for partisans, they ran us off. We went from house to house. We begged for food. We asked for information. Nobody would tell us anything.

We came to the last house. This was the end of the village. There's a woman in the house and she let us in, but she says she don't know, never heard of partisans. They're trained that way, because you never know who you're talking to, and she says, "You better get out of here, because if you don't, my husband's going to be home and he'll kill you." For the Germans to catch him giving us shelter, that's the rule.

The husband shows up, and she tells him that in the corner there's two Jewish kids. (The other one was not a kid, he was a man, but she called him a kid.) She tells him we're looking for partisans. He picks up his axe and he says, "If you don't leave, I'm going to chop off your head and put your head in the street and then you'll leave." Outside it's cold and it's snowy, and that's my first impression of the woods, and I've got no place to go. I'm not leaving until he tells me how to get to the partisans, and if he wants to chop it off, then let him chop my head off. I've got nothing to lose. The lady gave us two boiled potatoes to eat. We ate that, and out of the clear blue it's already almost dusk. Just before it gets real dark.

There's a man on a horse. You can tell he is a partisan because he has the red star on his cap and a partisan has a certain air about him. He walks into the house, he sees us and we talk to him. He thinks we're spies. He's not going to tell us anything either, and I tell him what happened, where I come from, and he says, "Machik." *Machik* means little boy. He says, "I can't help you. I can't tell you where the partisans are. But," he says, "it's snowing outside. If you think you're fast enough, follow the footprints in the snow. Now, the snow is going to cover them up pretty soon, so you better be moving. I'm not just going to stroll. I'm going to be riding real fast." He takes off and we go after him.

Just about the time we were beginning to lose his footsteps, boom, we're right smack in the middle of a camp. It's the place where the Jews from Dereczyn have escaped.

9. End of December, 1942, the Dereczyn encampment: I run into a cousin of mine

The camp has just now been through what they call the *oblava*, the massacre, a couple of weeks ago. You could tell—there was just the tents, the food hanging on the trees, fires being stoked away. A lot of canisters laying around. Very, very few people. Someone shows up here and disappears. Another one comes from someplace else, and I keep telling people who I am, where I'm from. They don't care. So finally one lady says, to me, "If you're hungry, get yourself a canister and boil yourself a potato." Well, my first night outside I tried to boil that potato, and it took me almost all night long. Potato never did cook. Everybody's water boils. Mine doesn't boil.

So finally I fell asleep by the fire and I got too close to the fire and started burning. So there goes my coat. Now I had a coat without an arm. One arm was fine, but the other arm was burnt.

I ran into a cousin of mine—Chajke—a daughter of my daddy's older brother. She was considerably older than I was, with two little girls, and she takes me in her tent. In the morning we went out and she said, "We got to go get something to eat." She took me to a certain place. There was a lot of meat hanging on the trees. See, that was the only refrigeration they had when you killed a pig or a cow. These food items were left over from three weeks ago, before the German invasion took place, and I took some of that frozen meat. But she looks at me, she realized what a liability I would be. She says, "You got to go to find your Uncle Benny." She says, "I'm just a woman, a widow with two little children." She really didn't want me—she didn't need another—but she did me a favor and insisted that I not stay in that camp. "Your Uncle Benny is in the other group who is more advanced in the ways of the woods, and there's more men over there, not just so many women and children." By nighttime, she finds out that there's a group heading in that direction, some going from the Dereczyn encampment to the Zhetl encampment. She puts me in touch with them.[5]

I'm following this new group and we walk all night long. By daybreak we came to a forested place with towers called *mayac*, which means tower. The foresters built them, for several reasons. One of them was for engineering, to know the lay of the land. Another one was for fire protection. My G-d, that's the worst giveaway if you're going to be hiding in the woods. And the tower is on a little hill. I looked around and I thought, "There's not a chance in the world that we can survive in this place. These people are stupid. What would make them build their camp right under the tower?" The answer was, "What do you know?" I thought I was bright but they ignored me.

But I come up and sure enough there's Uncle Benny. I don't remember what his reaction was, but from then on I was primarily with Uncle Benny.

My cousin George Bliss had been with him. He came from my daddy's hometown—Dereczyn—same place where Uncle Benny did. But he didn't want any part of Uncle Benny. He had joined the active fighting partisans in that area and became an officer. The partisans were originally Jewish farmers, and his mother, my aunt Minnie, had married into a farming family that owned a great big plot of land.

---

[5] She was killed two weeks later. The Germans came and attacked that encampment and killed her and her children.

10. End of December, 1942, the Zhetl encampment: a basement dug in the ground

I got there at the end of December. There were probably 6 or 10 what they call *zemlyankas*, basements dug in the ground and covered up. The walls were sometimes made out of branches of trees so they won't cave in, but in the wintertime you don't even need that because the ground is frozen and the top is covered up with lumber and then covered up with dirt, so when you get inside there's a hole. If it's twelve by twelve, there's room for, I don't know, fifteen, twenty people, everybody just sitting or lying around. It's warm; it's not freezing.

We were about 50 miles away from the Bielski brothers. They took almost everyone. You could go by yourself or you could go in a group. You could stay with them or you could leave. Those two took in strays, kids, relatives, nonrelatives. A couple of women were there. There must have been about fifty people in their group. They would not accept me, because I was not from their hometown. I would have given my right arm to be one of that group. You would tag along in the back until they would turn around and tell you to leave. They had hidden rifles. I stayed with them a couple of times, spent the night with them, but that was all.

In the meantime, there was a Jewish partisan group that controlled the area. After the Germans killed two-thirds of the Russian partisans, they came and said, "No more racial groups. We got to be integrated," and they took all the fighting men and they spread them around between their own companies. Some went with this company, some went with that company. But the anti-Semitism in those companies was out of this world. You would go out on guard duty and then they would come and kill you because they said you were asleep. If you were ever sent on guard duty, your chances of coming back alive was probably a third—you were going to get killed with a bullet in your back. The leaders were a Dr. Atlas and a Polish Jew named Wegweiser. But whoever the leaders were, they disappeared overnight, within two weeks.

So now the leadership is gone and the manhood has been separated out, and now we got nothing but a bunch of sick women and children.

11. Early January, 1943, New Tel Aviv and Ruda Yavorska: What it was, was typhoid fever

Several days later I walked out with Uncle Benny and we came to a place called Lapchiska, jokingly called among Jews, "New Tel Aviv." It was an island in a swamp about two hundred feet off the highway. The swamp is all around you and in the middle of it, there's a dry area. (In our staying in the woods, we were asked to move by the Russian partisans at least three or four times because we were too close to that island. Asked? We were *ordered* to move; by four o' clock you'd be gone. They didn't want to draw attention.)

New Tel Aviv was an organized camp. Most of the people who built it were already killed. They made baking ovens and now it's whoever survived using them.

There are actually doctors nearby. I think there were three doctors and about three nurses. They called it the hospital. The Russian partisans must have had about 30 partisans aside to guard them. The reason: in case somebody important was wounded, injured. I'm noticing people are frostbitten and I noticed that people are passing out into a coma. They just—they disappear. They sleep forever. Some wake up. Some don't wake up. What it was, was typhoid fever. Some people are absolutely not making a bit of sense. They're hallucinating. And this one is frostbitten. This one is sick. Then the doctors show up and if you're frostbitten, so that gangrene doesn't set in, they cut off your leg to where it's damaged. Now you know what chances you've got with a cut-off leg.

I am with a group going back towards Ruda Yavorska, to see
if they can get some potatoes, and there are, again, Germans in the
village. I've never seen them. They say they are. They're here, they're
there. Who knows?

By that time my mind is really shut. I think I was already sick. I
remember I had an incident with a dog. A dog chased after me and I
was scared stiff of dogs. I run. The dog catches me. Pardon me: I shit
in my pants, scared stiff. Then somehow there's a sled with potatoes
on it being carried back to the woods, and I ride on the sled and I
fall asleep.

My shoes are tight. I'm wearing very good shoes but they are
tight. I can't stand it anymore. Come to find out, my feet are swollen.

The doctor takes a look at my feet. He says, "You're frostbitten,"
and he comes back two days later and he looks at them again. He
says, "I'm going to cut off your left foot," and I beg him not to. He
doesn't care. He said he is not going to fight with me. "There are
people dying every day. When the gangrene sets in, then two days
later you're dead." I was looking in a couple of the baking ovens.
There were kids laying in the oven warming themselves—their legs
were already cut off. The doctor had them amputated, and they're
dying. And I said, "No, I don't want to end up like that. Let me wait
another day." Maybe it's not as bad as the doctor says it is.

And then it's becoming very, very, very hot. I mean I'm burning
up and a lady walks up to me. She introduces herself—she's my
daddy's cousin Chaya, and she says she knows me. She feels my head
and she says, "You got typhoid fever." Says, "You're finished. Not
only is your gangrene going to set in. Your typhoid fever is going to
get you." And she says, "Come over here." She's in a little half-base-
ment, about a tenth above ground. She says, "Come on with me,"
and we're sitting down there. And she says, "I'm sorry." She says,

"You're not going to make it. You didn't even have a chance." See they've already been in the woods for six months and I'm just a newcomer. She says, to me, "Now, if you had some gold or some money..." She just says that in passing. She says she knows somebody who could get us some flour. If she had some gold, she said, "Maybe I could nurse you out of this sickness."

I said, "It just so happens, you know, I do," and I take off my shoe and I say, "In the heel of my shoe there's a 10-dollar gold piece."

My daddy was well prepared for things like that. Everybody in our family had a 10-dollar gold piece in the heel of his shoes. You never know where you might end up. It's a good place, number one, to hide it and nice to have in an emergency.

She says, "You're already hallucinating." And I said, "No," and "Go ahead and try." I remember her yanking off the heel. She got the heel off and there is the 10-dollar gold piece. And that's all I remember.

Weeks later, I wake up. She tells me the story, that she took the gold piece, she bought a sack full of flour. She says, "You were out cold." She says, "I didn't think you were going to make it." She says, "This is how much flour is still left in the sack from what I bought." She says she had two daughters with her. She said, "We ate and this is what's left. I nursed you the best I could." She says, "I hope you've got another 10 dollars of gold in the other shoe. That's your business but I couldn't do anything about your feet. Let's hope for the best."

My Uncle Benny tells the story a little differently. He tells the story with a dream, that my mama came in my dream and told me to go. That is not important. Important things are facts, not dreams.

When I came out of my ailment, I hear people saying that Stalingrad fell. I knew there was a great battle going on at Stalingrad.

Now it's already beginning to thaw out. The snow is thawing out and I walk outside and I look around. I said, "My G-d. These damn Jews, they're stupid. They've built their camp right off the highway." You can see the highway from the camp. So certainly you can see the camp from the highway. The German army goes by on the highway, all they have to do is just step inside. So I hear that other people are saying that the camp was built at the end of the summer, when the greenery was real thick. They didn't realize the proximity was that great. In the wintertime, you're right within view.

Not only is that a bad place to be because of its location, it's also very low and, as the ground softens, all the basements flooded. Not only is it a dangerous place to be, you just can't be there.

12. Spring 1943, New Tel Aviv: Uncle Benny's got his one goal in his mind: he's got to find his old friend Feldman

I joined back up with Uncle Benny after I overcame my typhus. Uncle Benny was out of his element. He had gotten away from his own people to join another group, because he knew his own people disliked him so much, and deep down in his mind he had another problem, and now I come to another story.

In his childhood, he was friends with a man named Feldman. Uncle Benny was the man from the aristocracy. Feldman was the upstart, okay? Uncle Benny's mother was a widow; the Feldmans were now nouveau riche, they were getting rich. So Uncle Benny had it in his mind that Feldman was born with a silver spoon in his mouth, and Feldman was always lucky. Feldman got the pretty girl, Feldman made the money, Feldman built a big house. No matter what Feldman ever did, it was terrific. No matter what my Uncle Benny did, everything came the hard way. So Uncle Benny's got his one goal in his mind: he's got to find his old friend Feldman. Now, they were not really friends. They were both friends and rivals. Somehow he finds out that Feldman is in another encampment about two miles away.

We get up in the morning, we make the trek to that particular place. It's sitting in a swamp, but there's no tower over there. We go into the encampment and there are more organized little groups. Ten people here, eight people there. Again, nobody wants us. We've got nothing to offer. We're now three children (me, Marvin, and Florence) and one man, a wild-eyed man, who have nothing to offer.

What have you got to offer? You can offer two things. You've got to have a rifle. That makes you a man. Without a rifle, you're a nothing. But if you've got money or gold, you can buy a rifle or you can get someone to serve you with a rifle. Gold economics work everyplace, and meantime I'm begging. This one gives me a potato; this one gives me a piece of bread. This one says they knew my family, they have pity on you.

But sure enough, Feldman is there. Mr. Feldman left his ghetto. He found out about the woods. He got a wagon with a horse, packed most of his belongings. He came to the woods in full style. He didn't escape to the woods. He immigrated to the woods. He just moved there with a horse and wagon, with supplies, with a saw and an ax and a shovel. With blankets, pillows, lots of money—gold. And with this you didn't have to rob or beg, you could buy provisions. He arranged it, paid off people.

Feldman had teamed up with Robinovich, a forester, a woodsman who knew every corner, every swamp, every little creek of these woods. He was almost at home in the woods. I guess he had maps in his head. Robinovich was in reality a hireling of Mr. Feldman. They were both husky men. Robinovich was a tough, tall big man. Feldman was also tall, and good looking. So Mr. Feldman has a wife and two children with him, and the wife's sister and her boyfriend, and the wife's cousin with two children. Robinovich has a wife, Miriam, and two children, Ruth and Toby. There are other men with their girlfriends or wives. There was a group of about 10, 12 children.

They are living in high luxury, I'm telling you. They got pots and pans and blankets and clothes. They wash, they do their laundry —they are on a camping trip and we are naked. We are hungry and naked.

Uncle Benny says, "Children, there's one thing we are going to do. We are going to go where Feldman is going." If you stuck with Feldman, you could survive. Now Feldman and Robinovich threatened to kill him on several occasions, would take an axe and threaten to kill him. Number one he didn't have anything. Number two he had three children schlepping along. They let us stay, but we were always a little bit separate. Time was we were ten feet apart; other times we were a half mile away, a quarter mile away. Uncle Benny was always watching to see if they were leaving. Finally Feldman is moving out and my uncle gets the word. "Let's go!" Robinovich from then on became our navigator.

I was barefooted that summer. So was everybody else, but I had more trouble than them because I had to learn how to walk barefooted in the woods. And, not only that, but I'm frostbitten. I'm really in trouble moving. The snow is still on the ground and I'm barefooted. But somehow, during the day, the sun would come out and I would just get out in the clearing and get my feet out in the sun and I could feel the rays of the sun healing me. Would you believe it? I could actually feel it. And little by little I still had trouble walking for the whole summer but it healed. On one toe, the nail came off. But, other than that, everything returned to normal.

13. Spring 1943, Nakriski: how did we live?

And now our life in the woods begins, the real life. How did we live? It's the first spring. We were next to that village called Nakriski. It's a known place.

Food we didn't have. Occasionally Uncle Benny would go out at night in the nearest villages and get food—I don't know how he got it, whether he stole or he begged. He certainly couldn't buy it because he didn't have anything to buy it with. We barely got by.

Lice, you just don't know. The thickness of the lice over you, lice will crawl from one person to another just like that and they multiply. In one day, you got a whole colony. Uncle Benny really quickly figured out a way of controlling them, not 100 percent but well enough. Number one, you cut your hair. That's a standard in that part of the world anyway. You seldom let your hair grow out. The only time you let it grow out is because you didn't have a chance to cut it. The other thing is you boil your clothes. And from then on it became a standard with Uncle Benny, any time we had time and we had a bucket. And we built a fire and we filled it up with water and we'd boil the hell out of our clothes. Now, if you boil your shirt but not your pants, the lice will still survive. It's a constant ongoing battle but we fought that battle and we didn't control it but we pretty much minimized it.

On top of that, an ailment spread amongst us, characterized by high fever and delirium. It's very, very contagious. You don't have to touch me to spread that disease. If you touch that table and I touch the table, then I have contracted the same disease and it's terrible. A lady in that Feldman group was married to a pharmacist. Then Mr. Robinovich's wife owned a drugstore, where you sell soaps—she was not a pharmacist but she had some knowledge about pharmaceuticals. And the two of them got together and they remembered the prescription for that disease. The ingredients for that prescription contained alcohol and pine oil. Mr. Robinovich says you take the roots from a pine tree and you boil them in a certain way— "In that village, there's a place that makes pine oil." Finally we couldn't stand it anymore, and my uncle sends me and his son to the village to get some of that pine oil. We take a bucket with us. The Germans were on one side of the village. We were on the other side, where the pine oil factory was. We stole a bucket of unprocessed pine oil and we ran back to the woods. And that pine oil stinks one gosh-awful smell. But it cured it. Trust me it did.

Then the Germans established a barracks in that village and we decided that there's no point in pushing our luck. We left but from then on we were constantly covered with pine oil. Every minute. My Uncle Benny was a stickler for cleanliness and would rather be clean than fed. Another good thing about that pine oil was it deterred mosquitoes. We lived in swamps and mosquitoes were thick. They don't like the smell of that pine oil so it helped us. They weren't the only ones—we'd go out into a village to beg for food or rob for food and they would smell you. They just said, "Get away!" They can't stand your smell.

We moved to another camp. When I say an encampment: we're here today, next week we're three miles in a different direction, but somehow we kept in touch. We had an idea of where other people were. When it was quiet, we would walk over to them. See if maybe they had something to eat.

Now that gives you an idea of what life was in the woods, my experience in the woods. Aside from the time when I was sick with the typhoid and the other diseases, it was terrible.

How did we eat in the woods? Nobody's trapping animals—in the woods, I've only seen two snakes. As far as seeing wolves, not a one. As far as seeing rabbits, not a one. And the reason we didn't see 'em is I don't think they were even there. The woods were not that thick. The animals don't like to be around people. I've never seen a wolf and I've never seen a rabbit and I've never seen a bear. No sign of them either. Well, we did hear howling. Somebody was howling. Somebody might get a pig or a cow in the wintertime, and hang out the carcass on a tree so in the wintertime it will at least be frozen.

For some reason or other, we almost never found anything to eat growing in the woods. Occasionally, after rain we found mushrooms. Maybe four or five occasions. there's a certain mushroom that we know is edible. And if it wasn't that one, we didn't touch it. The kind of mushrooms—it's a little yellowish, with a square cap on it. The stem was about one or two fingers. And had a little cover on it, a little cap like two inches on each side. I loved them. But a rare occasion. And for some reason they don't come out except right after a rain. The rain is over? Two days later there ain't anymore. And mushrooms are not, have no eating value, no calories. You think you're eating something.

In season, we had these blueberries. There were certain spots where they grew rather plentifully. But that's only two or three days, and only certain patches. And the rest of the woods didn't have them. You'd pick the whole berry—it looked like a little red strawberry. They tasted great.

So you go out in the surrounding villages and you do the following. You either beg or steal or rob. Feldman bargained. He had money, just plain old gold. He would make a contact with somebody and he says, "Here's a twenty dollar piece. I want three wagons of flour brought in. I will take it down a sack at a time this week." They always had food. We lived next to them. We were starving but somehow we got by. Clothes—it's whatever the partisans got from the local villages by means of robbery. You go into a peasant's house and you don't have a shirt and he has one. You tell him to take his shirt off and you got it now. That's it. Same goes for shoes. The same goes for clothes. The same goes for bread. That's how partisans basically lived off the land.

Now, when I came to the woods, I was doubly dressed because of the cold. So in the summertime, I had extra clothes. I didn't wear all that. But in the wintertime, it was cold. I had burnt my sweater when I first came to the woods, and that's what I wore for the next two or three years.

I thought being in the woods was a lot easier for the kids who lived on the land, who lived in the small shtetls, who were more used to living in the field. To me, it was a great revelation. It was a lot harder to adjust, or at least, I felt that way. Most of us, aside from our short brief time with the active troops, lived a miserable life.

14. 1943-1945, the woods: I was not much of a partisan, but...

Now, there are a lot of heroic stories about partisans. I was not one of those heroic stories. Friends of mine were, but you're not here to listen to stories about my friends.[6]

When the Germans left the partisans alone, they used to regroup. Small groups of 10, of 20 or 30, would become 50 or 60 or 80. Then, 200. They would organize big camps. The Russian government tried to send paratroopers to organize them better because the Communist regime in Russia was jealous of any other activity that was not controlled directly by them. It was fine with us. It gave us some sense of protection. But the Germans used to come back in force and attack us.

The big attack took place before I got to the partisans. Thereafter, they never came back to us in that large a force. Number one, they learned that large armies did not cure it. Now, they had to bring in smaller, better-trained units to fight the partisans the same way the partisans fought them. For instance, they would find out where we were located and then attack us early in the morning. Come up to the camp and at daybreak, they would start their attack. I would say half of the people that were in the woods when I came, which were already probably one-third of the survivors from the

---

[6] There was a Polish Jewish boy that came into our outfit—into the Lenin outfit, which was a more elite group —and he led several attacks on German barracks. He single-handedly captured an entire company of White Russian volunteers fighting for the German cause. He just dropped in on them. He slit the guard's throat, came in with his little machine gun when they were asleep, turned on the light, and says, "Everybody quietly step out." Single-handedly led them all out. He too died later on in an act of heroism like that, in a stupid way, but he was the local folk hero.

original group, were decimated by small attacks like that.

I was involved in one attack like that. For some reason or other, I went to visit the Bielski group in a different location, a couple of miles away. It was headed by two Jewish men who took in a bunch of strays. I wasn't going to join them, there was no question that they'd accept me, but I spent a night in their encampment. They were gone. Most of them had gone out on an assignment. An assignment means they went to gather food. When we went out for food it was only at night. A woman and two kids were left behind, and I spent the night over there at the fire and then, in the morning, I decided that there was no point in staying there. Whatever I came for wasn't going to be, wasn't going to happen, and I got up at daybreak and left.

By the time I got back to my camp, the word was that that camp was attacked. Right before sunrise, the leaders and the older ones came back from their mission with food, and literally walked into a trap. There were several casualties. So that's how close I came. I was not much of a partisan, but I was part of them on several occasions. I always thought I had a better chance of survival with them. I joined so I could eat. That's the reason I was with it. When times were good and they could afford to have me around, which was not that often, they had me around—pulling guard duty, washing dishes, peeling potatoes. When I had to go on guard duty, they would give me a rifle. When I had to do an assignment, I would have a rifle. But then I would have to turn it in so someone else could go on guard duty with a rifle. On a very few occasions, I was sent on an assignment. I was with fighting groups four or five times. As little as a week, and as much as three weeks. Sometimes, they were very daring. Sometimes, very much in the open. You could not go on assignment to the local villages because the local villages were protected by us strictly for our own safety. We didn't want that population to be against us.

The few times that I was exposed to aiming at people, trying to shoot at them, I knew that I was not that good a shot. Because I couldn't see. And I said to myself, "I don't want to be a killer." When I pointed a gun and I had to pull the trigger I said, "I don't want to aim and kill anybody. Let somebody else do that. Not me." So I don't know if I ever killed anybody or not. I don't think I did.

One time, I was with an outfit that went out on an assignment. We went some place I would say 25, 30 kilometers away, and coming home, we had three wagons loaded with goods, loaded with food. We're not just hauling it back on our shoulders. It's nighttime. I'm sitting on the edge of the middle wagon, out on the rail with my feet dangling off, and the horses are just trotting one behind the other one. Suddenly, it got bright and I saw his face. I saw the German behind this machine gun, firing away at us something awful. And the horse took off—started galloping, and I lost my balance and I fell in the wagon. The wagon was not protection. The horses took off and that's how we got out of that one. Strictly by luck. I don't think the other wagons made it. I don't think so.

15. 1943 or 1944, the woods: do you see the boots on that guy?

We were out on assignment. A German convoy was going to hit a certain highway. We, the outcasts, the ne'er-do-wells, were sent to be the ambushers—to show you the Russian mentality, the most important assignment they assigned to the dregs. We had to watch the road to give them the signal that the German convoy was coming. I think we laid there two or three days in that hiding place and one morning, there is the German convoy, led by their scout.

One of our group, who was a recent recruit, a local peasant, he's lying there with his rifle. He says, "Do you see the boots on that guy?" And he loads his rifle and he shoots at him.

The Germans stopped, figured out where the shot came from. I guess they spotted us. They surrounded us and tried to flush us out. Those who weren't killed right away, I don't know how many there were, but some of us took off running. I mean, there's nothing to lose now. I'm running with my little rifle and I trip and fall. I knew the German was going to catch me and I cocked my rifle and I put it under my chin and I was going to shoot myself not to be caught alive. Didn't have the guts to do that either; not that much of a hero. The German came up, kicked my rifle out of my hand, peed on me, and walked away.

About 30 minutes later, I got up, and I picked up my rifle. I realized I was wounded. I tore off my shirt and put a tourniquet on my arm. I knew that much to do. I got back to camp. I was not the only survivor. One boy came back unharmed. One boy came back with a terrible wound in his stomach. He later died.

That was the end of our big ambush that naturally was a big failure.

16. Fall 1943, the clearing in front of the swamp: a pair of shoes

The second winter, we were already more intelligent. We sort of knew what we were doing. We lived on the edge of a big clearing, about a kilometer wide and a kilometer long, woods on all four sides of it. Right behind us was a thick swamp, impassable. There was nothing to the left, nothing to the right, nothing behind us. It was just not passable, so we only had one way to go: you had to go frontwards. Mr. Robinovich, the guy who was Mr. Feldman's henchman, picked that particular place because it was inaccessible. The mere fact that it was sitting at the edge of a clearing said you'd have to be insane to build your hiding place there. Behind us was an impassable situation. He always played the strategy game. Very sophisticated.

And in that area, there must have been about six or seven of these little groups, but everybody, like we did, followed Robinovich because they knew that he was the local man. We spent the whole winter in that area.

Then we realized there was no point in hiding. If they spot you, they'll spot you whether you're on the ground or not on the ground. So we built a little tent above it. In the middle of it, you could stand up.

We got ahold of a field stove, an iron stove, that did not have a cover on it. You could build a fire in it but you had to have a bucket on top so the fire wouldn't be blowing out. In order not to burn it up, we boiled water constantly. So we always had boiling water. We boiled our clothes. The heat that it produced, when it was producing, was out of this world. Our sleeping place was behind that little stove. So if it wasn't windy, we were all right. If you sat on the other side of the stove, you were freezing to death. It was pretty well concealed—well, if you got within 10 feet of it, you would know we were there because it gave off so much heat.

I was with Uncle Benny and Marvin in slightly elevated places in the swamp; mine was right next to theirs. You could walk in between. And then there was another cousin of ours. Right by the doors, an older lady. Chaya. She's the one that spotted me before I got sick, said she was my daddy's cousin. I never knew her before that. And she's the one who said, "You got typhoid fever." And she's the one who looked after me while I was out. And she somehow joined with us. She had two daughters.[7]

Sanitation, you know everybody had their own urine container or bottle with you and when you're hiding underground, sanitation was right there with you. For your thirst, you had to pace yourself. So you couldn't drink any water because your bottle would get filled up real quick. You learn how to do these things.

Next to our room, we dug another little basement where we kept our food, a little hideout hidden under a bed. You could access it only from the inside of the encampment. We had flour there. Robinovich and Feldman built an oven where they could bake bread.

Other than the group of Feldman and Robinovich and us, there was a man by the name of El Yasha and he came from the village next to the woods—Ruda Yavorska—where I was going to when I escaped from the labor camp. He had a wife and a sister. He was a farmer. This was a big brawny guy—he would carry his mother

---

[7] Both of them perished with the partisans. They went out on an assignment to fight and they got killed.

on his shoulders any time they moved. And his mother had a little bitty pot that you could boil one potato in. And she kept kosher. They ended up in our encampment. It was Robinovich facing this way and then my cousin Marvin and I built our little group facing them. Probably less than 10 feet apart. And behind us, El Yasha came and he built his hideout maybe a foot or two feet in the ground and the rest was strictly above ground. His tent, so to speak, was about 20 feet away from us.

And about a quarter of a mile away, some people built a place like Robinovich did, to house 15 or 20 people. But they never used it. They decided it was too crowded and they went someplace else. But there was a lady who had two daughters, and when she realized that there was an empty place, so she didn't have to build, she moved into that 15-unit deal. One of the daughters was a hemophiliac, and I think she had a walking problem too. The girls' survival was serving the troops, the partisans. They were very pretty and they never did join a fighting unit, and anybody wanted to have a good time for the night came in and brought their sack of flour or their strip of bacon or whatever. They took in two boys. One of them was my age, and had the name Chaim Weinstein. And he came from Ruda Yavorska. That lady took in that boy out of pity and he was more or less the houseboy. He would clean up and bring in the wood or what have you. They could keep warm and it was room enough for 20 people but it was only those five. The mother, the two daughters, and the two boys.

So this boy comes running to me and says, "Tevi, there's somebody looking for you." Who would be looking for me? So I go over to see, and there's a man on a horse. I mean, a heroic-looking figure, a big brawny guy with his machine gun strapped across his chest. I walk up to him. I says, "You looking for me?" And he says, "What's your name?" I told him my name. He wanted to know my daddy's name, my mother's name. He says, "Yeah. You're the one I'm looking for." He said, "I want you to know I made this trip, a 100 and some kilometers, just to see you and pay an old debt." What the debt was, I don't know. I think my daddy might have—my mother may have acted—some act of kindness toward his family. The best I can remember, he was a porter. He would take merchandise from my daddy's wholesale house and carry it on his back to the railroad station for the retail merchants. Anyway, he says, "I understand that you are barefooted and it's wintertime and you need a pair of boots." So he says, "I brought you a pair of shoes." And he gave me a pair of rabbinical shoes. They were five sizes too large, but that's not important. With the slip-on style and the high heel—stylish, I was not. And then he took out a slab of bacon and he gave me a loaf of bread and he says, "Thank you for letting me pay back an old debt. I've accomplished my mission." Then he just took off and I have never seen him again.[8]

So with those shoes on, I survived the second winter in the woods, not having to be barefooted and not having to be frostbitten.

As time wore on, we were heavily surrounded by the Germans. The Germans figured out where we were going, which pass we were taking, and they would come at night and ambush us. Just the way we used to ambush them, they started to ambush us and it was impossible, impossible, to go out to get food. The front was already close to us. You heard the artillery, but you didn't know what was going on because, we were pretty well cut off from the world. We knew something was going on.

If the Germans had the manpower and wanted it bad enough, they could find us because there were tracks in the snow and the more you travel in the snow, the more you walk, it's right there, it's a footpath. But they didn't come that winter.

---

[8] I made enquiries about him after the war and the people that I talked to did not remember him. Where he was, where he came from, I don't know. Only thing I do know, that he came from 120 miles away to do this particular act of kindness for me.

17. Late fall 1943, the swamp: building the hideout

About a mile away from our regular camp, we built a special hiding place. Robinovich and Feldman had the idea, then they realized that we were going to be watching, me and Uncle Benny, and we would join them. So they decided to let us build the hideout together. Robinovich knew how to do it. My cousin Marvin, Uncle Benny's little boy, about a year younger than me—he was very handy with tools. Uncle Benny not only wasn't handy with tools, he hated any kind of work. So I was supposedly the muscle with Marvin. And he knew how to build it. And we watched what Robinovich did and we tried to imitate it or improve on it.

Ted pointing to hole similar to an in-ground hideout

Entrance to in-ground hideout, now potato storage

Theirs must have been something like, oh, I would say 12 by 30. After they got through building theirs, my uncle sent me and my cousin Marvin to ask him if we could borrow their shovel and their axe and we built ours. Ours was probably 6 feet high by 8 wide by 10 long, and approximately four feet in the ground. It was a hole in the ground about four feet deep. We couldn't find another place that wouldn't draw water. We were in the swamp.

We dug out the sand. We had had plenty of time to prepare for it. We carried the sand away so it wouldn't be noticed that there was some digging going on—we carried the sand little by little in little sacks. I would say it took us four or five weeks. *Zemlyanka* is the word for it. *Zemlyanka* means it's in the dirt, in the earth.

We put a cover on the hole, with lumber and vegetation and grass growing over it and leaving one opening, except that opening was well-concealed. That opening had a bush growing on top of it. It was just like a planter. When we wanted to really hide it, the last person would move the planter in and rub garlic from the local farms around the sides. Dogs do not like garlic.

You couldn't live in it. The little basements that we used to build were made to live in. And the hideout was meant to hide out in. In other words, you couldn't stand up in it—you could sit up. It had room for about 30 people sitting.

18. Winter 1943, the camp by the clearing: he gave us a pair of boots

Another time, we—Uncle Benny and I—were going someplace to get food and as we were going, on the way back, we weren't carrying anything. He smelled a still. I always kidded him—he was a drinking man, and he had had a liquor store. He made an abrupt right turn off the trail, and I kept hollering at him, "Where are you going? This is not the way back!" And then we came across the still, and there was the moonshiner himself. Polish. We waited a while and the whiskey started coming out. The first drips are a lot more powerful than the last ones. I tasted it and it almost killed me. Must have been 90% alcohol. That's about 180 proof. But we had some German currency, and somehow we walked away with a few liters, each about the size of a quart. We could trade whiskey.

The whiskey wasn't clear. It was muddy. A lady in the encampment was the widow of a pharmacist. She showed me how to filter it. You take a birch tree and you make coal out of it. And you grind up that coal and you run the whiskey through that coal and it comes out clear. But it has to be only from birch coal. Pine will not do it. You could drink the birch coal to help dysentery, too. There were quite a lot of birch trees—we always had to be where the trees had leaves, and not pine needles, for cover.

Some partisan wanted a drink and he gave us a pair of boots and that was going to be our commodity in trade for a quarter of a quart, or half a quart. Meanwhile I was going out to one assignment. I went to one camp, spent the night over there, and I got up in the morning and every inhabitant of that camp was gone. I came back to my own camp and then my uncle told me a story about the boots:

Somebody snatched the boots, or anyway they disappeared. And then my Uncle Benny went on a wild goose chase to see if somebody saw the man who had the boots. And he carried on all kinds of ways. He's getting worried. He's following in his mind where the boots must be and he tells me I need to go to such and such a place to get the boots and I take off to do as my uncle instructed.

I go to the first house, the second, the third, the fourth, and then, I'm going into this little place, this single farmhouse, which is en route. And I walked into the yard of this single farmhouse and I saw two horses. By that time, the riding horses were already long since disappeared. The only thing you had were some old nags that could barely pull the plow. I'm looking at these two horses. They did not look like plow horses. They looked like cavalry horses.

I decided not to walk into the house. There was a little summer stable—not a barn, but where they kept the horses overnight in the summertime. It wasn't really protected, but a temporary shelter, and I walked in there and I thought, "Let me rest up before I go in the house." And two Germans walk out of the house and they're fixing their horses to ride wherever they were going. And I'm standing there in front of that barn, I'm not even hiding, and I guess they noticed me. They take off their rifles and start aiming at me and I take off. Behind that little barn was a pasture and all the shooting broke loose, and I'm just running for all I'm worth. There was a little creek and I remember jumping into that creek and the bullets hitting the water. I knew they were after me. Anyway, they didn't get me. I got out of that creek, kept running. They kept shooting. Then, there was a little wooded area and they stopped. I never did get to my destination or find the boots.

A couple of hours later, I got back to my camp—but our little encampment was gone, the one that was at the edge of the swamp, and then I really panicked. See, the problem around there is you didn't know where you were and you didn't know where you were going. No maps. No sense of direction—And I waited all that day by myself in the swamp and it was scary. I mean to tell you, it was scary. I ended up spending two days all by myself. I didn't want to go to the special hideout because I didn't want to expose them. In case I was being followed. The second day there was still shooting going on. But when the shooting stopped, I decided to make a run for it. I went towards the hideout. I didn't know if they were there.

I went into that place and that's where my people were.

19. January, 1944, the woods: Shlomo

Now comes the story of my cousin Shlomo, who I'd gotten separated from when we first went to the woods. My cousin Shlomo also
had been in New Tel Aviv. He had teamed up with three or four other
Jewish guys from a town called Zhetl, and they joined the fighting
unit. And my cousin joined it as a water boy, so to speak. He became
the mascot of his unit. Although he was Jewish, he was the number one volunteer for railroad assignments and his specialty became
blowing up railroads, and they would assign him either alone or with
somebody else to go. You got to find a spot. You got to plan it. You got
to make sure you find out what the railroad schedule is and it takes a
couple of weeks' time to blow up a railroad. He had eight trains to his
credit.

I used to see him periodically, every two to three weeks, once
a month. He told me some very unusual stories. Some of them I
believed, some I didn't. He went through the typhoid fever, so he
might not have made any sense because he was affected by the
disease. But he was completely reckless.

Then he disappeared for a couple of weeks. He might have
been affected by the fact that his mother was killed and he was
a person driven by revenge. He made the trek all the way to the
Bielskis. And there were some people in the Bielski group—I don't
know, a woman or a man, a husband or something—who had
somebody in our group, about 100 kilometers away. For the price

of a 5-ruble gold piece, my cousin promised to lead him back to this camp. He used the money to get a rifle. Now that he was a man with a rifle, he was welcomed back into his unit.

I told Shlomo about the gold and other treasure my father had buried in the backyard. I said, "In case I don't survive and you do, then you should know what is where." And I mentioned certain places to him.

Now it's January, 1944. The word is that a German troop train is going to pass the railroad between Grodno and Lida. It's a secondary line and it's got to be blown up. And the leadership has organized a contest. Several groups were going to go out, assigned to different areas, and he and another boy, one of the other four, went off on their assignment. They blew up the train and they were on their way home. And they were crossing the River Neman. It's a big river over there. You don't just walk across it; you got to take a little canoe, a boat, to cross it.

At the crossing, they met up with some of the other competitors in the contest. There were eight to two. The eight of them said to lay down their rifles, and Shlomo and the other boy said, "We were taught never to lay down a rifle." And after exchanging a few words with the others, Shlomo and his friend were shot. The other boy was pretty beaten up in addition to being shot. Shlomo was just shot in the head.

They brought him back. They buried him under one of these towers with a great big marker called "Geroy Sovietskogo Soyuza." That means "Hero of the Soviet Union." Stalin never gave him the medal but the local commander put up the marker.

That's the story of Shlomo. My son is named after him.

20. Spring 1944, the special hideout: we lived on raw rye

We had all the Robinovichs and the Feldmans and us in the hideout, and there were some others. There must've been perhaps 30 people in it. Some who did belong. Some who were freeloaders who came in to hide.

We'd go out at night, but at daybreak, we'd get in the hiding place, put the cover on it, and spend the rest of the day in that hiding place. We had holes dug for ventilation, and were always afraid that the dogs might spot us through those, and then the Germans combed the woods.

We had almost no food to eat. Hungry. We couldn't bake because the little baking oven was destroyed.

We found some sacks of rye, and we hid it in our encampment across the clearing, the place that we would go to at night. It was where we kept the flour before, and it looked like it was part of the wall. At first, actually, we thought it was poisoned. But then after we tried it, we ate it. At night, we would build a little fire and try to cook. We had a little pot, and put water in the pot and then put the rye in it and tried to cook it. It was still not edible. (We could have a fire because the Germans didn't go into the woods at night. They were afraid! As far as they were concerned we had arms. A few did, but not in this encampment.)

So we lived on raw rye. Now, it's nourishing, but you can just eat so much raw rye.

It was days on end that we just didn't have anything to eat. I've seen some that were starving. You could tell they were not going to survive much longer.

My little cousin Marvin and I, we always talked about getting a hold of a frying pan with bacon and fried potatoes. Potatoes. You either boil them or you put them in the ash. And they bake in the ash. To this day I think it is the greatest dish. Boiled potatoes … is a luxury. Potatoes, you can make a soup out of potatoes.

But potatoes themselves are not that nourishing either. It's the rye that's nourishing, the bread is nourishing. Potatoes is just a filler.

The Germans didn't attack us in the winter.

In the spring, it's a different story. In the spring, they did come. They came to our encampment while we were in the special hideout. They went through the woods arm to arm to make sure that they didn't miss anything. They literally walked on top of our hideout.

You can imagine the trepidation, and we know it's almost the end. And they just walked on by, hollering and screaming in German.

There were Ukrainians with them, and the dogs barking, but they never did find us. And I told you, we put garlic around, because supposedly dogs don't like garlic. They threw grenades in some of the camps (not in ours). We had some potatoes dug in the ground for storage purposes and they even spotted that and poured gasoline on it so you couldn't eat it. They sprayed the places with gasoline and set them on fire.

They never went inside the encampment, so they never saw the little space under the bed with the flour.

After that day, we thought they weren't going to come back again, but we didn't know. So we got a little bit more brave.

There were attacks constantly. With Mr. Feldman's luck and Mr.

Robinovich's skill, we avoided most of the attacks on the surrounding areas.

21. Spring 1944, the special hideout: news

The only way news came to us was by word of mouth. The word got around—people who used to go for food in the villages used to get whatever news they had. And they never had the right news. But you could tell. What's going on? As the armies got closer, the Russians were attacking and the Germans were retreating. You could hear the artillery from almost a mile away. When we first got in the woods, the war had been 900 miles away. But the front kept getting closer. People were leaving our area.

I was in the hiding place and a man came by and he says, "The Germans have retreated." My uncle says, "We've got to go get something to eat." So, danger or not, we walked about six miles to a village. We're starving to death and could barely walk.

The Russian peasants have what they call a hand mill, which for years have been prohibited by the government, but every farmer had their own: One great big stone on top of another one, and you turned that stone by hand, got a little handle on it. And you grind your rye into flour, so it became edible. And it's the hardest way. We went to a house with that. We brought our own rye and the woman was still in the house, the children were gone, her husband was gone, but she was in the house. And she let us use that grinding stone and we must've tried for three hours to grind up maybe a handful of flour to bring back. She did give us some old sour milk, with two potatoes, which tasted like the greatest delicacy. We came back to camp and we cooked that rye flour into cakes.

The next morning the same guy came back, and he says he was just on the highway and there were Russian trucks passing by. "How do you know it's Russian trucks?" He says he saw the signs. At first we didn't believe him. So we sent out another man to see, and he says they had the great big signs on the truck and they were speaking Russian and they said something to the effect "for Lenin, for Stalin, for the homeland"—you could tell Russian propaganda, "Berlin or Bust." So we took his word and took whatever we had in the way of belongings and we walked out of the woods to the highway. We were still really in the woods, except we got on a highway. A Russian truck passed us by. And the second or third one, we more or less hitchhiked. One of them stopped and said, "Y'all need a ride?" "Yeah, we need a ride." That driver took us on the truck.

That was it.

We had spent about 30 days in the special hideout.

Part IV: LIBERATION

22. Spring 1944, Dereczyn: there's no Jewish part of town anymore

The Russian truck took us into town. It wasn't our town or my father's hometown. It was the town where the people we spent the time in the woods were from. It was Zhetl—the county seat of my mother's hometown.

We spent two days in that town. And we didn't have any rights in that town because we were not from there. Before the war, it probably had had a Jewish population of 3,000. A non-Jewish population of probably 2,000. About 5,000 people in it. When we went into this town, how many Jews were there? None! Two thousand Polish and Belarusian people. They pretended like nothing happened.

A couple of days later we took a 100 kilometer trip to my Uncle Benny's hometown, Dereczyn. My uncle realized that Dereczyn was further west, and it had been liberated.

There was no Jewish part of town anymore. There were probably four or five groups of Jews, maybe 25 Jews left. My uncle's house was burned, my grandmother's house was burned. We ended up with my uncle's neighbor. Who was not particularly welcoming, but we wanted to eat. That's where Marvin and I fixed the bacon and potatoes that we had been dreaming about, and I got sick. I was sure I was dying. There was a Russian lady doctor, and she read it exactly: "You just ate too much!" The next day I was fine. After that episode, I watched what I ate. How much I ate. Even though I was hungry.

Then later, my uncle found a former Jewish house that was occupied by a Polish family. For some reason or other, they did not occupy the whole house. They kept themselves to the two back rooms. And there were four rooms in the front, that were empty. So we moved in there. The Jewish people that had lived there were dead. The Polish people didn't have anything. They were not farmers. They were city people. I think he used to be some kind of a clerk for the local government. We lived with them for about six months.

There was plenty of food in town. Just like normal times, the farmers from the surrounding area used to bring butter and eggs and honey and what have you. My uncle got the job of running the local mill that milled the rye. So we had plenty of bread. 'Cause that's the way the milling operation always worked. One tenth of what you mill goes to the miller. That's the miller's fee.

The German money was no longer worth anything. The Russian army came with their money, but you couldn't buy anything with it. I mean, there's no stores, there's nothing. It's all a question of bartering. If the farmer brings butter and eggs into town, they want to get something in return—want to have a shirt, going to get a pair of pants, or they want to buy flour with it. We had flour to barter with.

I was a good student before the war, and now I tried to enroll in a Russian high school. I had made it through the sixth grade, and I wanted to enter the seventh in a certain school that I wanted to go to, like a high school, in the next largest town, 25 miles away. I was hoping to board at the school. They denied me admittance. "High school is closed for you." That's one way we knew that the Russian government was no longer friendly to us like they were before the war. Somehow Stalin changed everything. They said I should go back to the woods and try to teach the peasants how to read and write, that I would do much more good for the country than I would by going to school myself. Naturally, I didn't. I went to work in that mill that my uncle ran.

Next to the mill was a little house, a little shed. The chief partisan from that area, his name was Bulak. Before the war, in peacetime, in the '20s and '30s, Bulak had been a Communist in hiding in the woods, a partisan. The Polish government suppressed the Communists, so he was a local Communist hero. That was his claim to glory. When he came to town he did not get into the Russian army, and he became the head—the president, the mayor, the chieftain of the town. He and Uncle Benny used to sit in the shed and drink whiskey. Somebody had to operate the mill.[9] So that's what I did. It was a great big chimney, about 10 feet high, and you had to feed it with wood from the top. The chimney powers a great big belt, and that belt is probably 20 feet away. And 20 feet away is the grinding stones. The belts operate the stones, one round stone on top of another one. The wheat, the rye, gets fed in between—then it becomes flour. It was loud! I was making sure the fire was constantly burning

My cousin Marvin was at home. He was a domestic guy. He just loved raising animals—he had rabbits, he was trying to grow Angora, it's a certain fine wool. He didn't raise any vegetables. But then he had chickens and then we had a cow. And we had a horse. He was running a farm. I was about 14. That made Marvin about 13 and Florence about 11. Florence was always with us—she sorta did the cooking and woman-like chores.

---

[9] To this day, I don't understand how the mill worked. The belt comes from a power source. I don't know where the power source was. The miller comes in and feeds the wheat in. There's a man who takes care of the stone. He gets paid with some flour, but not a tenth. There's an art to milling. One stone just turns over another one and it's got to have ridges in it. So it can mill it. Every morning before you start, he knocks out the ridges. Same stone every day but the ridges get milled down. They flatten out. So the stone, slowly but surely, gets thinner and thinner and thinner, to a point where it's no longer useful. And that's what the worry was: where were we going to get the stone replaced? It's a specially-made stone.

23. Winter 1944-45, Dworec: digging for Winestone's gold

I was very, very depressed. I did not know what was happening.
School would not have me. I didn't know where I was going. A
deep, deep state of depression set in, and I did not want to go back
to my hometown, my mother's hometown, Dworec. I did not want
to go to visit graves. I just didn't feel like it. But my uncle insisted
on me going back. His brother-in-law came to visit us, Benny's
brother-in-law, Meyer Bakalcheck, and he was a railroad employee,
and conversation got around to it. "Oh," he says, "no problem." Says,
"I'll take him to this particular Dworec. This train runs this way. You
catch the train that way." So we got on the train.

We came to Dworec, and I go to the house where we lived.
Remember, I told you we lived in two rooms, one room on one
side of the street, and one room on the other side of the street. The
side of the street that we were kicked out of survived. The other
one was burned down because it was in the labor camp. So I knock
on the door of the existing house, and asked the lady for a shovel,
and for permission to go in the backyard. And she says, "Go ahead."
And I start digging and there is my 55-gallon drum with my daddy's
things. And I pull them out, and I go someplace else in the yard. I
knew exactly what to do, and this lady is baffled. I cover up the hole,
and I thank her very much, and I go away.

But first she gave me my mother's fur coat, which my cousin
Florence wore until she decided that it wasn't stylish, and a leather

briefcase that my mother had saved for my bar mitzvah.

I go across the street. This is the funny part. Across the street where the house burned down my daddy buried gold in the basement, and I was there when he did it—on purpose, I suppose. So I go across the street, and the house is burned, so now it's an open basement. I take the same shovel, and I start shoveling the snow out of the basement. And I'm digging, and a neighbor comes up, and he introduces himself. He remembers me, my mother. Could he help me? I said, "Please." And he takes his shovel and he helps me dig the snow. We dig up the snow, and I go to the spot where I knew the stuff was, and he says, "What are you digging?" And I tell him, "There's something here that I need to find." He says, "Are you looking for Winestone's gold?" I said, "How do you know about Winestone's gold?" He says, "Every surviving Jew from their town that came to visit went to that basement to dig for Winestone's gold." My cousin Shlomo had told everybody—he being probably off his rocker, or being reckless. The word spread. So he says, "You're wasting your time. They've already probably found it."

But I'm already here. I might as well keep digging, so I dig, dig, dig, dig, dig. I knew it was under the foundation, and I had it in mind that it was two feet underground. I miscalculated. But I found it! It was two and a half feet. Maybe it sank, I don't know. When my shovel hit the can, I pulled it out. The wrapping that the can was in had rotted away. I opened it up and there it was, and now I'm a millionaire, literally, and I'm taking out the first gold piece, and I tip him. And he says to me, "Son," he says, "with all that's happened to you today in this town, you're gonna be dead by nightfall. If you're not gonna be robbed, people will kill you out of jealousy. If the police come, they will certainly confiscate it and kill you. The best thing you can do is get away." And I thought, "That's good advice," and I got away.

24. Early 1945, Dereczyn: apparently you and my friend, Teddy, have a problem

I went back to my uncle's hometown literally a millionaire. Not only did we now have clothes, and made clothes with jackets, and pants, and all kinds of things, but I had a jar full of gold, too.

A man showed up from my hometown by the name of Koso. *Koso* means goat. He comes to visit me and he says, "We got to talk." We go through the pleasantries, and he says, so and so survived, and so and so survived. He said, "We got to build a monument in that hometown." I said, "True." I thought about it quite often. I said, "Why don't you and I get together. We'll contact everybody." He said, "Oh, no." He said, "You are going to do it by yourself." So I said to him, "Why me?" He said, "Because you found Winestone's gold." I said, "How do you know about Winestone's gold?" And he says Shlomo told him.

So he's got the facts all right, and I figure this way. If I admit that I have the gold then this is going to be an act of blackmail forever. Today it's the monument. Tomorrow he wants to take his girlfriend to the beach. It's a forever thing. But if I don't admit it, then who's going to build a monument? And he'll probably call me a liar and report me to the Russian Secret Police, because the possession of gold is against the law. I am just in a terrible state.

A little boy in that town, also a survivor, walks in the house. I wasn't quite friendly with him, but how many of us were there?

Probably less than half a dozen. I was about 15 at the time. He's probably two years younger than me. He walks in the house and he says, "Teddy, you're white as a sheet." I said, "That's right." He says, "You've got a visitor. He's giving you trouble." And I say, "That's right." He says, "You would like to get rid of him, wouldn't you?" I said, "Oh, if I never saw him it would have been the best thing in my life." He said, "No problem." He walks outside. About 30 minutes later he comes back with a rifle. (Apparently, as the armies moved back and forth, he got ahold of a rifle and by that time we were already educated that you had to have a piece of something to protect yourself with, and he had buried it in his barn.) And he uncovers his rifle, cleans it up, and he walks into the house. He says, "Uncle, you are going to the railroad station." The uncle is not an uncle, but that's the way you address him, and he says, "Says who?" And the boy says, "Says me and my Springfield rifle," whatever they called it. He jams the bullet in the chamber, and he says, "Now," [and] points it at him. "Put your coat on."

And the man puts on his coat, and the boy says to him, "Now, let's have it understood." He says, "I don't know why you're here." This is a nice, little bitty kid. He says, "I don't know why you're here and I don't want to know. Apparently you and my friend, Teddy, have a problem. So if something ever happens to Teddy, you are responsible. Makes no difference what, when, or where. For the rest of your life, anything happens to Teddy," he says, "you're responsible. I will come and kill you. And if I won't kill you," he says, "you see this boy across the street? He will come and get you, and down there there's another boy. We're all part of the same clique." They didn't exist. "He will come and get you." He marches him 13 kilometers to the railroad station, puts him on a train, and Mr. Koso disappears out of my life.

I have not seen Koso since, but I never built a monument, and I had mental problems because of that.

25. April, 1945, to the Russian Army to Dereczyn to Poland: everything is going to be great

Upon liberation at the end of the war, I went into the Russian Army. Everyone was drafted and I thought I was a big hero and I went with them. Whether they wanted me or didn't want I was there. I ended up at the Russian front, maybe a couple of days or a couple of weeks and got sent to guard German prisoners after the war. For about 30 days, I was sitting in a caboose. Every other Russian freight car has a caboose attached to it, a little booth. And the prisoners were inside and we were going east to some German POW camps to deliver the prisoners. When I delivered them they told me to go home. And I had no home to go to. I'm probably 15, 16. I went to find Uncle Benny.

The war wasn't over yet. The handwriting was definitely on the wall that you better get out. Jewish people needed to go to Palestine. Poland was being liberated, and the Russians said to us, "If you consider yourself a Polish citizen, you have an opportunity to go to Poland. Otherwise you're going to have to live in Russia as a Russian citizen." And from Poland, keep going closer to Palestine. Because we were born in Poland, we could do that. After a lot of soul searching and consulting with other people, we decided to become Polacks and move to Poland.

We went to Poland probably around March or April of 1945. We went as farmers. We took our cow and our horse with us. We were put on a freight train and we come to a strange city, and my uncle gets up in the morning and we're still on the railroad car. He goes to see what's going on. We don't even know where we are. We were delivered. We are on the track, and he says, "Everything is going to be great." I say, "Why is it going to be great? He says, "The next car is Feldman."

We met up at the railroad station, and my uncle and Feldman from then on were inseparable. Robinovich was away. Feldman did not need the forester, and the forester wanted to do different things. They separated. And Feldman and my Uncle Benny became partners, and friends—always arguing—they had a strange relationship.

We settled in a big city called Lodz. It's the second largest city in Poland. Two-hundred thousand non-Jews, and by that time, there must have been a couple of thousand Jews. Lodz was a central point for everybody to congregate. There was a Jewish committee. That had contact with Israel. But the anti-Semitism in Poland was even worse than ever.

Uncle Benny started dealing with cattle in Poland, buying and trading horses and cows. First we sold the horse and the cow for a pig and sheep. And he is a good trader.

Then there's German cities being liberated by the Russians. The Germans abandoned their homes and retreated further west. And for a couple of months, almost all you had to do is travel to Danzig or travel to Breslau and take whatever was in empty houses, whatever homes have left over in them. Sheets, or clothes, or shoes, or utensils. Things that you could barter with. Then get back to Poland and sell it and live off of that. I did that once or twice. My cousins went. Poland now is beginning to have money, a different currency called *zloty*. Russian currency is still good because the soldiers are still there.

There were plenty of empty apartments in Lodz. I was still

living with Benny and my cousins. And Feldman and his family.
We had one room and they had one room. We stayed there until
September.

26. September, 1945, Lodz, Poland: cousin George Bliss with all his medals

One day, four or five Russian officers come to our doorstep. One of them was my cousin George Bliss, with all his medals across his chest, the hero, he won the war with his colonel and his major. My cousin did not spend the war years with us in the woods—he was in the fighting outfit next to us. He later became my mentor, guardian, protector. He survived the Russian Army. The life expectancy of a Russian infantry man was probably three weeks, very brief. Most of the partisans that got into the army were wiped out the following month on the front. They were always replaced by others. You just don't know how many people there are in Russia. The reason for George's success story was that he had linguistic ability. He could speak German because he took it in high school. Also it's close to Yiddish. So he was the interpreter any time they would catch a German prisoner. His colonel kept on promoting him from the ranks till he became a captain.

The Russian Army had given him a week off and he came to visit us. The war was over, and his division was being transferred from Germany towards Japan. George hadn't stayed with us. But because I knew how to write and I was inclined that way, I communicated with him. So he knew where we were.

They're coming in and they're having a big, big party. Everybody was drinking, toasting each other, the victory. My uncle says,

"Where're you going?" The Russian soldier says, he's "going to
Japan." See, the war with Japan wasn't over yet. Benny says, "What in
the hell are you going to Japan for?" The Russian says, "We've got
to conquer Japan." By that time they're all drunk, and then they pass
out cold.

My Uncle Benny says, "Take George out in the barn and let
him sleep on the floor." So we picked him up, [and] we carried
him into the barn. There was a lot of hay in the barn, [and] we put
him in the hay. He was an animal lover—I mean he was strictly in
his element. Then my Uncle Benny asked us to go see how he's
doing. He says, "Get him undressed so he'll be comfortable." So we
undressed him.

In the house, little by little his commanding officers came to,
and they each rambled on back to their unit. When Cousin George
woke up, he said, "Where am I? Let's have another drink," and he
passed out again. By the time he finally came to, it was five hours
later and he was a deserter. A deserter from the Russian Army faces
death.

We got him papers, false documents. We gave him some civilian
clothes and we took him to the railroad station and shipped him to
another city in Poland where he had relatives. But about two weeks
later, he came back and joined us.

The Polish passed the word for the Jews to move on, that
Poland did not want them. One morning the Polish police came
knocking on our door. They shot up the apartment with bullets,
made us all stand against the wall, and they said they were going to
machine gun everybody. My cousin George and another brother-
in-law of my uncle, who was also a deserter, when they saw the law
coming they broke the windows and ran. I'm telling you not just
plain windows—iron grates. I mean the strength of running away.
They ran on the roof. They got out of there.

Meanwhile the Polish police did not kill us. They just threatened us—they lined us up against the wall and fired over our heads. And they said [in another language], "Jews go to Palestine." We went to report it to the police the next morning, and whoever the policeman was on duty said, "They told you right. They gave you good advice." With that type of a message, we knew that it was time to go.

27. September, 1945, leaving Poland: we were Greeks going home

There was no place else to go but Palestine. Every place had gone through the agony of the war. Poland was occupied by Germany, just now liberated. Czechoslovakia was like that, Romania was like that, Hungary was like that, Germany wasn't even liberated yet. And of course we were strangers in those other places. In Poland we could speak Polish. But to go to Czechoslovakia, it's already a different country.

America, there's Canada, South America—that was not even a thought. We did not have any connection with the Americans. Anyway, liberation is in the eastern part of Europe. Germany is still existing and fighting the war. And the Americans are on the other side. So you can't get there—it's impenetrable past this. You have to go to Palestine.

We ran down to the Jewish Committee, started snooping around and asking, and they said, "Yes, there's a way of getting out of Poland to go to Palestine, but it's a long, tedious way. Are you ready?" We said, "We are ready." They said, "You got to pay 300 American dollars." We had that money—we had dug it up with the gold my father had put away. We paid them.

We packed up. Once we got signed out, they had an organization that told you what to do. It was very secretive: Report to the railroad station at 11:00 on Wednesday, then some girl or some men will walk by and say, "Take the train to Krakow." Not talk to you, just pass by. We did that. Looked around, somebody came up to us and said, "Take this trolley, the number 4 trolley, and go to..." —not a hotel but it's something like a hotel. It was just a dump. Report over there. Next thing you know, somebody tells you there's a kitchen on such and such street, that offers free food, you go there and they tell you to go to Katowice. Another town in Poland. And that's how we traveled.

We were going south from Poland. Greece being south of Poland, we were Greeks going home. In order to be Greeks, you had to pretend that you did not speak Yiddish, German, Czech, or Polish, didn't understand any of it. Don't tell them that you understand them. Do not answer any questions, act strange. With the cap being turned backwards, the shirt turned around buttoned from the back, your socks inside out, any oddity that you could possibly think of—to indicate that we were strangers around there. We didn't dress like them. Some men even wore skirts. When the authorities stopped you, you looked straight at them in the face and if they talked to you, you didn't understand and you knew not to give yourself away, you recited the Kaddish or whatever prayers you knew by heart from your child-hood. Most of us knew the Kaddish, unfortunately. They don't know Hebrew. So they'll leave you alone.

That's how we rode the trains. Because you were not allowed to travel as Jews. We've got nothing. No papers. No tickets. The 300 dollars, that didn't pay for tickets either. You just went as a Greek. The conductor used to come ask for the tickets, you stand up there and you recite the Kaddish. If he kept talking to you, you recited it again until he gave up. So, the hell with him. You could say, "Athena" and "gracia, gracia." You say what you say. You are who you say you are. What's the conductor going to do with you? "Give me the money or get off the train." He ain't man enough to do it. We're forcing our-selves on the train. Local conductors were either Polish or German.

And they didn't want to make trouble.

September is when we started acting as Greeks.

28. September, 1945, Czechoslovakia and Austria: start speaking German or Yiddish or whatever you want to

From Poland, we came in to Czechoslovakia, a town called Bratislava. We spent two weeks over there in another organization camp. Bratislava was already more accessible to Western influence, but the Russians were there, too.

And, then, little by little, you could tell different groups were being transported further south into Austria. In Czechoslovakia, the same group, the same mysterious direction one day a man comes around and he says, "Pack up. Tomorrow morning, be at such and such place. Take train number 29," and that carried us to Katowice, Brno, then Bratislava, then Vienna.

We spent a couple of days in Vienna, maybe a week, and then the word came to cross the Danube by boat, a little rowboat, still as Greeks. Austria was split between American, French, English and Russian areas. We ended up in the American zone. They took us to a place, a displaced persons camp, which was a former concentration camp. It was not one of the death camps, but it had barbed wire. They told us to take a shower to get deloused. And none of that Greek: Y'all start speaking German or Yiddish or whatever you want to.

I don't think we stayed there more than two weeks.

From then on, we were under the auspices of displaced persons camps, which were not the greatest places to be either. Sometimes, you had food, sometimes you didn't. The hunger situation in Europe after the war was very persistent. That's when I became educated in the ways of calories. A person requires 1,800 calories to survive; we were getting 650.

29. October, 1945, Bad Gastein, Austria: It's a resort area!

Ted, Phillip Lazowski in Bad Gastein

In Bad Gastein refugee camp. L-R: Willie Moll, Ted Winestone, Phillip Lazowski

Next a truck came and took us to the Austrian Alps, an exquisite resort area called Bad Gastein. And we walked into this fancy hotel. All five of us—me, Benny, Marvin, Florence, and George—were assigned a room. And we stayed there a year and a half. We were there probably October through the following December. About 13 months.

It's a resort area! It's a fancy resort area. I think they must have had 1,500 Jews in Bad Gastein. Occupying five hotels. During the war, the beautiful hotels had been converted into rest houses for the German Army. If a soldier was wounded, and they gave him 30 days' recovery period, they sent him to these hotels that were converted into barracks, with double bunks.

There was no food, except the American Army supplied basic rations. They would feed you twice a day a little soup, a little this, a little that. On holidays we had fancier food. I was still hungry. We would try to go skiing. I knew skiing from my hometown. And I disliked it then. The reason I disliked skiing was, where I come from, it's flat. So you got to go and learn how to cross-country ski. And that's a lot of heavy work. And for what purpose? I always thought, you pay a lot of money to hurt yourself when you can do it for free. In Bad Gastein, I used to go up on the ski lift, which was very pretty.

They even organized schools for kids and in that school there was one lady who spoke English and tried to teach us English.

30. Fall 1946, Italy: never in your life did you ever dream of such places

Getting towards fall in 1946, my cousin George and I took
a trip from the hotel in the Austrian Alps to Italy. With a sack
full of cigarettes to smuggle them. We walked over the mountain
through the Brenner Pass and crossed the Austrian-Italian border.
We ended up in Italy in the morning. And then we got on the train,
the same way, traveling to Milano. And then to Rome. And then
cousin George, besides speaking German, was familiar with Latin
and French. French was a desired language. And he walked up and
down the train saying, "Gee, I can speak Italian!" He started talking
to people, of course they realized that he was not Italian. And then
the conductor came with police, and arrested us, and put us in jail.
The jail ended up being an empty basement. The house above the
basement had burned. And we spent the whole night in jail and
in the morning somebody was supposed to take us to court, to do
something, but there was nobody around. They took our cigarettes
away and dumped them. But we didn't know that. We got out of the
jail and snuck around, caught another train to go south in Italy.

We went through Rome. We thought somebody was chasing us,
but my cousin made sure that we went to all the places in Rome that
he wanted. He knew about it. He was a high school... didn't graduate,
I think he was a senior or something like that. And he would always
take me to these places, [in] which I was bored stiff. He says, "Never

in your life did you or your ancestors dream of being in places like this. So absorb it! Get yourself civilized!" We were there a couple of days. George was educating me. We went to Milano. He took me to a concert at La Scala— "Never in your life did you ever dream of being such places…" We had Austrian schillings but they accepted it.

We ended up in Bari, in south Italy, on the beach. We enjoyed it—we ate oranges. And then we realized that nobody was looking for us. And we traveled back home, back to the hotel in the Alps.

Not fearless. Careless. *Don't give a damn.* They catch me, what can they do with me? Other than feed me?

31. December, 1946, Bad Gastein, Austria: wherever they send me that's where I will go

My cousin George Bliss got us to America. Their family were big landowners, and they had a sad history of the oldest son taking the entire estate. For three straight generations, there were 10 sons in each generation. Well, that's an oddity. There was a Jewish nemesis by the name of Haman; you might probably know about Purim. Haman had 10 children, and they were all hanged. So, their nickname was the "Hamans"—Jewish people have a funny sense of humor. So, now you've got three generations of Hamans, only one of them ends up with a homestead and a lifetime of unhappiness: if they were one out of 30, the other 29 were their enemies. Most of the rest of them ended up as farmers, in Canada, which still offered land to settlers. After the war, my cousin George put in an ad in the Jewish paper in New York City that he is Joe Bliznianski, later Bliss, and from so and so.

One of his uncles replied, and, he said to him as follows: "I am your uncle; I still carry a big grudge. I have not forgotten anything from before. Neither me nor my brothers will help you. It's out of the question. We've sworn forever—but," he says, "the situation being what it is, I will try to introduce you to other people who could help you."

This Bliss person, George's Canadian uncle, who rejected his family, contacted my father's brother in Brooklyn: Herman. He says, "Your people are alive, and here's where they are. I cannot help them. I have sworn them off." He says, "You do something about it." And

Herman said, "I will." At that time, he was a house painter who had just fallen off a scaffolding. He was painting the Loew's Picture Show in New York, and broke every bone in his body, and he was being hauled around in this cast.

He wrote to us and told us that he was going to do everything in his power to help us. Now he went from household to household, from cousin to cousin, traveled to Boston to places to find out, see if anybody would guarantee our coming to America. Uncle Herman remembered there was somebody from his brother-in-law that came to visit him some time ago—an old lady who lived in Brooklyn, not too far from where he lived. To him she was a fancy lady. He contacted her. He told her that her nephew was alive and would she do something about it.

I get this letter in Austria that she's my Aunt Tillie, and she is glad that I have survived, and she would like to help me. I didn't know I had two Aunt Tillies. All I knew I had an Aunt Tillie, and I know she died, got killed, so I'm—hey, what's the difference. Let it be Aunt Tillie, or maybe she's a cousin of the other Aunt Tillie. I don't know.

L-R: Rivka's Brothers – Chaim Pinsky (Ruleville, Miss., died early)
and Ben Pinsky (Ohio)

This Aunt Tillie went to work for me. This Aunt Tillie found my mother's brother Pinsky, in Bellaire, Ohio. This Aunt Tillie had a very, very wealthy sister, my great-aunt Hinda, in Mississippi. Make a long story short, when we got to America, this Aunt Tillie passed the word that "that one," meaning me, she's in charge of. The others—Benny's kids, George Bliss—were different cousins. They did not have any connection with her, so she took me.

I had no plans or desires to come, none whatever. I didn't have any place to go, but wherever the powers that be would send me that's where I would go.

Back when I was in school, it was embarrassing when the schoolmaster would walk in the classroom and say "Rabinowitz, Klein, Schmidt—go home," kicking out the kids who didn't have money. I never intended after that to go to school that was not free. I heard that in America school was for free. That was the only reason I came to America. I did not know if I was going to be able to go to school, but I knew that I would not get any education based on tuition because, number one, I didn't have any money! But also the embarrassment of discussing tuition with anyone.

Then the word came to us that we're going to America. Because of Herman and Aunt Tillie, the authorities in Bad Gastein told us we had permission to finally travel to America. We were told to go to Bavaria, then Munich which we did and proceeded to have physicals and wait our turn to travel by ship to America. Somehow my lung X-rays were misfiled and I was told I had TB. Benny, Marvin and Florence traveled on to Bremerhavm to wait for a boat. George insisted on staying with me to straighten out this mess. George contacted other doctors for more X-rays to prove this was a mistake. This we did (because we had the money to do so). A re-examination showed my lungs were clear. We were again cleared for travel. George and I were then told to also go to Bremerhavm.

Because we were single, we were given priority and we left for America a bit before Uncle Benny, Florence and Marvin. This travel from Bad Gastein to Bemerhavm took about three weeks. They put us in a German military camp. We were pretty well fed—some American girls were running it, Red Cross volunteers. My English was about 60 to 100 words. I could say, "I want to go." "I am hungry." "Can I eat?"

Again, the papers were cleared. Herman finally got the papers together, and he brought all five of us to America: Uncle Benny, his kids Marvin and Florence, George Bliss, and me. Immigration recognized brothers and sisters. So my Uncle Benny was a brother to Herman who was in America. He was accepted, so he was allowed to take his family. Which included me. I then became his "son." He said I was his son. That was his contribution to our well-being. And the other cousins, we have a lot of cousins in America who came forth and they sent me papers. My mother even had a brother in Ohio who sent me papers. It means that they agreed with my request to come to America. That they will vouch for me—they will support me, and make sure that I won't become a ward of the state.

Part V: AMERICA

32. End of January, 1947, Brooklyn: Tillie was the family

We had cousins in Boston who invited us to a wedding. And we went to Boston: me, George, Uncle Benny, Marvin, and Florence. After about a week I made the decision to go further. My Aunt Tillie was more ... wanting me. I left Boston and went to Brooklyn. And they stayed in Boston.

I finally got there, and I see this old lady, and she—I don't know her. I don't remember who anybody was. I was not that observant to begin with, and now this lady says she's my aunt, which aunt, what aunt? What happens in the morning? They're going to find out I'm an imposter. Now where do I go? I don't even know where the other uncle lives.

I had very, very much a sleepless night, I'm worried about being an imposter, and the train tracks are running overhead and it's noisy, and the fire engines. I said, "Holy smoke, what's going to happen? And suppose the Germans come in the morning, which way do I escape?"

I wake up in the morning, and I look outside the window, and in Brooklyn they hang their laundry in the yard, from the second-story window. And I'll be damned, Hotel *Gayoso* is all over the clothesline. So that's my people! I still don't know what Hotel Gayoso is.

So now I'm with my Aunt Tillie in Brooklyn, who now I realize who she is, that I'm at least home, not an imposter. By and by over the years I figured out that there were two Aunt Tillies: the other one—I know she got killed—and this one. As mean and as nasty as the other one was to me, this one was like an angel, couldn't do enough for me, looked over me, hovered over me. I was the apple of her eye.

But she was a very, very poor person, extremely so. Tillie was not close to Hinda but she depended on her sister Hinda for support, even after Hinda died. Her apartment rent was 51 dollars a month, and the annuity that her sister established for her was 50, so each month she was one dollar short. I'll give you her economics. She rented out a room in her apartment to "the boarder," and he paid her 15 dollars a month. When I came she raised him from 15 to 16. That made all the difference in the world, and that was her way of life.

Ted's documents for U.S. entry

When I came to America she went to visit her brother and her niece and said, "I didn't receive anything from my sister's estate and I want my annuity." So they raised her annuity from 50 to 75 dollars. And then she said, well, what about the boy—me? And they set her up with 50 dollars a month for me to continue to go to school. I went to school and I worked. When I started working, I paid 40 dollars a month for room and board.

She married another man. Her husband was a religious Jew who could not hold a job for more than a week at a time, because he would not work on Saturday. The system was if you don't work on Saturday, do not bother to come in on Monday. He worked in the garment industry—a week here, a week there, maybe a month. But there was no steady job for him. Even in the Brooklyn garment industry, you gotta work on Saturday. They pooled resources. He was just as poor as she was, but outwardly you would never have known. She wore her sister's mink coat to church, and spoke with that very aristocratic, casual way. She knew how to play it, and her hair was always just spotless. She was one hell of a fine person.

She was the family. She held the family together.

33. 1947, Brooklyn: I did what every American did

Aunt Tillie enrolled me in high school: Thomas Jefferson High School in Brooklyn. I was interviewed by this woman, head of the English department, by the name of Agnes O'Hara Hayes, who wanted to know how much English I knew and how I would fit in. She wrote out my schedule in high school and she called me in after three days of testing me. She said, "I want to make an American out of you. But it will be a lot of hard work and are you willing to do it?" I said, "Yes."

And thereafter I did my part, and she did her part, and there was nothing unusual. I had to go to work—all America goes to work. What's unusual about that? I had to ride the subway three times a day, so you know, nothing unusual. I did what every American did.

High school was supposed to be four years of classes, or eight semesters. Mrs. Hayes assigned me to the third semester and then she wanted me to go to summer school but I missed that. When I came back and they wouldn't take me in, she said, "I'll tutor you." And she tutored me and when I got through with that, she skipped semester five and put me in semester six. And then she skipped seven and put me in eight. So I only went three semesters of the actual eight, but I progressed rapidly and did everything I needed to do to graduate.

Eventually I met people like me. There must have been 60 or 70 refugees in that class. I became friends with a couple of them.

When I was in the eighth semester of high school, which is the second half of the senior year, everybody was taking tests for colleges. So I rode with them. And that's how I started applying to college. I thought all the colleges in America were also free, and I took the test first, before I knew about tuition. I didn't know about scholarships. I didn't even know how to register—it was very confusing to me. But I applied. I thought, "Gee whiz, you're not going to NYU or Columbia," but I applied anyway.

Graduation was held twice a year at Thomas Jefferson High School. The graduating class was split in half: one graduated in January, and one in July. Our graduating class that July had 800 graduates. It took two days, in a great big auditorium. Every graduate got only two tickets. I brought Uncle Herman and Aunt Tillie.

Ted Winestone at high school graduation, 1948

We went out to an ice cream parlor in Brooklyn to celebrate. Everyone wanted to know what I would do next. It became embarrassing because I didn't know! It was set for me to become a house painter, like my Uncle Herman. Then a neighbor who was there suggested that I should apply to the fire department. My Uncle Herman wanted me to join the Marine Corps. Another lady from my uncle's side said to join the Teamsters' Union and become a truck driver—I didn't know how to drive. And then it came to my Aunt Tillie. She says, "My husband's son-in-law is an accountant. They do quite well. Why don't you be an accountant?" It stops the conversation. I say, "Yes, that's what I'll do." The conversation starts again and we finish our ice cream.

By and by, I got a job helping a truck driver deliver eggs and cheeses to various New York restaurants, and I worked all summer long. The job used to start at six in the morning and we got done about two in the afternoon and I'd take a bus and go home. I was drawing 40 dollars a week and I was a big shot. After two, I would go to Coney Island on the beach. But then the summer was over and the driver tells me that my job was about over because I was substituting for all different people who had taken summer vacation.

He says, "What you gonna do? If you were smart you'd go to college. But I guess that takes money. And you got to first pass the college exams—that's the way in New York." I said, "I did!" He looks at me kind of strange and asks, "When did you do that?" I said, "Last spring. When the semester was over I applied to different colleges." He says, "But all of those colleges cost money, except for CCNY." I said, "I applied for that too." He says, "You applied for CCNY?" He says, "All summer long I liked you, I liked working with you, I liked what you did, I trusted you, and now you start to lie to me." I said, "I did not lie to you." He says, "Of course you did." He kept on talking like that and he says, "If I find out that you lied to me, I'll make sure that you don't get paid for the rest of the week." Finally I convinced him. He made a U-turn on either 2nd or 3rd avenue going south and went north to CCNY—over 120 blocks. A long trip. Finally we're getting to the campus. He parked on the grass (that stuck in my mind). He says, to me, "Watch the truck. I'm going in to check." After about 30 minutes he comes out and says, "I owe you an apology—you've been accepted!" (Only about 5% of high school graduates get in.) He keeps apologizing for accusing me of lying.

We drive back and he says, "I want to do something for you. I want to talk to the boss. I want you to be my helper and rearrange my schedule so by two o'clock in the afternoon I can drop you off at 23rd Street in New York (a branch of CCNY). You can go in the back of the truck and change clothes and go to school. But I got to have my boss's approval." Two days later he said the boss wholeheartedly approved.

That's how I started to go to CCNY. I was already two days late for registration. And now I started going to classes. I signed up for 15 credit hours (which is five classes per week). A little over two weeks after signing up, I get a call to report to the dean's office. I reported and the guy says, to me, "Your registration is still wrong—you didn't fill out the registration properly." What did I do wrong? "You haven't designated your major." I said I didn't want to go in the army. He says, "No no no—it's not the army." He explained to me what a major was. I said, "What you got?" I remember the expression. He gives me a list of majors. Right on top was accounting. I said, "That's the one!" He looks at me and says, "You haven't signed up for any courses remotely related to that major." I said, "Do I have to?" Anyway, he got convinced that he was talking to somebody that was not aware of what was going on. He says, "It's already two weeks into the semester. I can't change your courses now." He says, "Next semester I'm going to make up your schedule."

Second semester he made up a schedule all over New York. They would have evening classes in high schools. I took two CCNY courses at Stuyvesant High School. And then Monday, Wednesday, Friday I would go to the School of Performing Arts.

I didn't go to a regular campus. He signed me up for five courses. I made the dean's list both semesters and then I went to summer school. And he insisted that I take a speech course. There were certain sounds I couldn't pronounce. Most non-native speakers cannot pronounce the "th," and I pronounced it either with a "d" or an "s." Like the "d" and "t" get mixed up. New Yorkers even today can't say *third*. They say *tird*. Most people like me couldn't pronounce an "r" and I can't pronounce it today. Like "Robert" —it sounds right, but it's not right.

Six months later, in the summer vacation I was invited to come to visit the family in Memphis. I knew I had an uncle in Memphis but I didn't know where. I knew the city was situated right on the second biggest river in the world, but I forgot the name of the city and the river. So I came to visit, and I'm told that you got to go see the old aunt, Hinda was her name, Mrs. Kaplan at the Gayoso, Gayoso Hotel. And I go up there. There is this great, big hotel with a sign, "Hotel Gayoso." I said, "Wait a minute. Does she own the Gayoso?" No. She doesn't own it. Anyway, come to find out she was a resident of the Gayoso Hotel, and when she was making up the big bales to be shipped to the poor family overseas, she would stuff the towels and the pillow cases from the hotel as extra baggage and *that's* how my family became identified in my mind as Hotel Gayoso. That's the Hotel Gayoso story.

I worked in the garment industry my third semester in college. The union did not work on Saturday, but I was not in the union. I worked for a supervisor who normally did not work on Saturday either, but in his mind I owed him Saturday. I probably came in less than 10 Saturdays, the others I got away with not working on Saturday. I was uncomfortable working on Saturday, but I had to do it. Very uncomfortable, because the tante didn't know I was working. She thought I went to some kind of synagogue. So I would get up in the morning and disappear and then make sure to come home at about 12 or 1 o'clock. She never asked me where I was—she had a feeling.

I lived with her two and a half years and as far as I am concerned, it was two and a half years of another mother.

And then one day I came home and my aunt had died. That was in the third semester of college.

Her husband wanted to sell the apartment. But it was not his. He had the right to stay or to sell the lease to the apartment. So I had to leave.

I called my Uncle Israel in Memphis and asked him what should I do. "Do you have money for a ticket?" I said, "Yeah." He said, "Get on the train to Memphis immediately and finish out the third semester here." So that's how I came to Memphis.

34. 1949, Memphis: they took me in like a son

It turned out that Aunt Tillie had saved all that money. The 50 dollars that she received from Hinda's estate for two years, and the money that I gave her for room and board, she put in a separate account. So when I came to Memphis I was rich. 'Cause I had about 10,000 dollars when I graduated.

I had 36 or 38 credits in courses. Uncle Israel never told me what to do. I signed up at Memphis State University.

I got a job at Thom McAn shoe store. Room and board didn't cost me anything in Memphis. I stayed with my uncle—he had remarried—for eight years. They took me in like a son.

Uncle Israel had been the rich man in Baranowicze. He came from Europe to visit his brothers and the World's Fair in 1939. He came to Memphis, not as the poor man but as the rich brother. He brought money. And right after '39, there were people in Memphis who had relatives over in Europe and there was a secret way of sending money to people in Europe. Israel's second wife, Dora, used to give people money in Baranowicze, and their kinfolk used to come and give the money back to Uncle Israel. Israel and his wife were rich people but everything was taken away during the War, except for the gold which they had hidden.

The Korean War broke out after my first year in Memphis. That was 1950. I was subject to the draft. My draft board was originally in Brooklyn and they would not talk to me or answer me or tell me anything. Most local people got deferments. I was still in college but they would not give me a deferment. So I would attend school with the idea that the next semester I would be in the Army. With summer school I got my degree in three years. I had to attend certain Saturday classes, but I didn't write because it was Shabbos. But I did finish, and then I went back to Brooklyn to talk to my draft board. "What happens? Are you gonna take me or not take me?" But got no answer.

I came back to Memphis and got a job with Bert Bornblum, who had a clothing store.[10] He asked me very plainly: "Are you subject to the draft?" And I told him, "I am but I can't figure anything out." And he quizzed me again and again. That was in November. Originally he wanted me for the Christmas season. November 15, I got a notice from my draft board, and I had to go. And he took it that all this time—the three or four weeks that I worked for him—that I had lied to him (even though I had said I was subject to the draft). I made up for those weeks for the next four or five years. I would work for him when he was busy. I would take my vacation and work for him at the store. Finally, he became reconciled that I had paid my debt. I had a degree in accounting and then I went into the Marine Corps.

---

[10] Note from Laura Helper: "In his interview with me, Ted actually said, 'Bert Bornblum, the one with the school.' I looked him up, and learned that Bornblum had himself escaped Nazi Poland in 1938 and ended up in Memphis, where he owned clothing stores on Beale Street and throughout the city. His obituary says, 'In addition to giving money to help build the Bornblum Jewish Community School on Humphreys, he also set up an endowment that means every student at that school will receive a healthy gift to offset the tuition. The Bornblums—Bert and his only surviving brother David—also founded the Judaic studies program at the University of Memphis while also making donations to the philosophy department. They donated to LeMoyne-Owen College as well as Southwest Tennessee Community College.' The obituary also quotes Bornblum himself: 'I never went to high school,' Mr. Bornblum said in a 2004 interview, 'but I read a lot of philosophy as a kid in Poland. That is how I got my education—philosophy became my primary subject.'" http://archive.commercialappeal.com/news/memphis-philanthropist-bert-bornblum-dies-2c4f69f4-164d-5b24-e053-0100007f5e06-369593931.html

Ted Winestone, 1950, in the Marines

L-R: Uncle Benny, Cousin George, Ted

L-R: Ted, Cousin George, Cousin Marvin Weinstein

I got in the Marine Corps when I was 21. I used to go not for seconds at meals, but for thirds. At the beginning I probably weighed maybe 128 or 129 pounds. I was still hungry. What changed was that it was available! In the service I didn't have to watch myself. There were others who were going for seconds. I won't see these guys again—in two months we'll be separated. When I got through basic training I came back at 179. I had gained almost 40 pounds. I caught a lot of hell because my uniform didn't fit right. One day it fit and then a week later it no longer fit. And they are very strict in the Marine Corps about your uniform fitting.

I came home on leave and my aunt Dora (Uncle Israel's wife) sat me down and she said, "I know what's happened to you." Before you went in the service, you tried to be civilized. You tried to sit at the table and be like a human being. And I watched you. And I knew what your problem was. Now that you know that you've got plenty to eat, *stop it!*" And we sat down and we decided, no more milk or cream in your coffee. No sugar. No extra bread. Definitely no pork, and small portions of meat if you can. Little by little my weight went down. To this day I see food, I go out of my mind wanting to eat it.

Ted with Uncle Israel and Aunt Dora Iskiwitz

Part VI: THEN AND NOW

35. December 28, 1942, Dworec: this is the day where the ghetto was liquidated

Then the story goes a little different. In about 2000, the new millennium, a Jew in New York calls me to refresh my memory.[11] His name is Yoselofsky.

Ted and Yoselofsky in 1997

He was not one of the privileged ones. His family was killed off. He was a Jew in a town far from Dworec who was conscripted

---

[11] Ted actually said "last year" in the interview, which took place in 1996. I took out the specificity to make the structure work.

to come to our labor camp. He was assigned to live with my family in our house. Apparently, he knew my daddy from before the war, and maybe my daddy asked for him to be assigned to us. My mother really took him in, got him a blanket and tried to feed him. He was about 25.

His brother stayed with us too, and he befriended me. He was about 18, 19. I was about 12. And sometimes at night, we didn't have any lights. We would take pine branches and strip off the needles—the branches would burn for about two minutes, then you would light another one. We'd sit in the dark and light the branches and we would dream about the days when we could go out and we would become farmers, because a farmer always has something to eat. The first year in the Russian school I had taken agriculture, so I knew academics about farming. And he knew practical things about farming. We were dreaming about the time when there would be plenty to eat and where we would dig up the potatoes, and have so many pounds for the rest of the family during the year, and then we would trade off. All these agricultural dreams.

In America, Yoselofsky (the older brother) found out about me. He came to see me twice, called me on the phone about 100 times. He says, "Your daddy built the wall where I hid out." He had a perfect memory. He knew everybody. He knew everything about me—knew about my likes and dislikes, and my relationship about living with an elder aunt that I didn't like, and she didn't like me. I mean he was a very observant person.

So he is my eyewitness, although other people have told me the eyewitness story also. I was outside the camp, so I didn't know what was happening. He tells the story this way. This is the day the ghetto was liquidated.

He says, till 12 o'clock, the camp was surrounded by Germans. And till 12 o'clock nobody knew what was going to happen. Mr.

"Schindler," in the company of three other SS people, called in Mr. Novich—the top Jew in camp, a relative of ours. He was a Polish Jew and he spoke German. Mr. Schindler and Mr. Novich had a very close interpersonal relationship. Mr. Schindler said to him, "The jig is up, I cannot help you anymore. Call the following people to get on the first truck to be loaded off." My father and mother were among the first. My daddy was made one of the supply people, and that's why he was called off by name to be one of the first to be hauled away. And he says, this guy Yoselofsky says, when he heard that, when he saw my mother and father being hauled off, he ran back to the house.

This was the first time the Germans used gas trucks, where they would load up the truck with people, and then the truck would go to the ravine. The van was air tight, and the fumes would kill you within five minutes. By the time the truck got to the ravine everybody in the truck was dead. They would throw the bodies out and go back and get a new load. And that's why we outside didn't know, because we didn't hear any shooting. Up until then, we knew that when Germans were liquidating a town, there was always a lot of shooting going on, and this was very quiet.

There was not a crematorium, and there was not an action of shooting. The whole act of killing the entire 2,500 people must have lasted three, four hours. By dark, in the wintertime, if the action started say at 1 o'clock, by 3 o'clock or 4 o'clock, it was over. The entire camp was liquidated.

Meanwhile even though Mr. Yoselofsky and his brother weren't supposed to know about that wall, they figured it out, and they forced themselves into that hiding place in the house that my father had prepared, to hide out. That place was already jam packed with people. He says there were 29 of them in that hideout while everybody was being hauled away. My brother Noach was there, my aunt Rachel was there, one of her sons (Elijah) was there, Manya was there. He mentioned to me all the people who were there. I can't imagine squeezing that many people in there. I can't imagine Tillie being there.

He said when the first day was over, they went out at night when it got quiet to catch some fresh air—they were suffocating— and to see if they could find something to eat. And he says, my aunt Rachel said to him, "You're a young man, you need to make a run for it. See if you can escape." She says, "We are older people, we are women and children. You should not stay with us." He said to her, "I don't know where to go. I don't know how to escape." As if she had any power, she says, "I'm not going to let you back in to the hideout." Basically, she forced him out, after a long conversation. He and his brother and two girls made the break and they escaped. He tells me, "Your daddy built the hideout for me to hide out, and your aunt made me escape from that hideout to survive."

Other things I know from local people.

When the German came to kill my grandmother Sara, to haul her away, she said, "Not on your life. Nobody kills me." She grabbed his gun and struggled with him. A lady in her 80s had the guts to jump up and fight him for his rifle. How true that is I don't know, but that's the way the local people told us.

The next day, the townspeople tell me, the Germans burned down the labor camp. They figured there might be somebody hiding out in some private hideouts like that. When the house caught on fire, my brother and the other 20-some people ran out, the Germans caught them, shot them, and supposedly threw them in the well. Manya and Noach got killed with my aunt Rachel. So my brother survived by two days.

"Mr. Schindler" failed us. When the SS division came by our town, they were on their way back from a partisan action. And as they passed our town, whether they had orders or not, I don't know, but they liquidated the town, and Mr. Schindler didn't have the guts enough that the real Schindler had, to bluff them out any further, and he gave up. Although protecting us was definitely his intention to begin with. Whether he was making money on the deal, or he was just having a good time staying out of the army, I don't know.

Several things I remember about my father: he always preached not to mix with politics, not to mix into civic affairs, not to get involved in any public institutions, unless you were prepared to take a beating. The reason I'm telling you that is because towards the end, right before he was killed, he had to take just the opposite position to what he believed in, because we had money. When my mother decided that if we could feed 2,000 people, by her taking the chance and her paying for it, then she was going to do it, and she did. As a consequence, my daddy was appointed as the supply officer, or director, for the labor camp that we were in. I think if it weren't for that, he may have had a better chance of surviving. By being a known quantity in town, the Germans picked him up right away. In fact, they asked for him to board the first—this is not something that I've seen; this is what was told to me—gas truck, to be gassed and hauled away to their death. That's what happened. My mother and my father together were the first ones to be hauled away.

36. 1990, Dworec, the woods, Dereczyn, and Baranowicze: it was a tough trip

When Joscelyn and I went back for a trip to Rome, I knew every place. I knew the streets, I knew the Vatican, I knew there was where Mussolini used to hold rallies, the Tivoli fountains, yes.

After the Russian state disintegrated, I decided to go to Dworec, and I went. It was very disappointing. The old structures don't really mean anything. Most were gone. The church was still there, but a church doesn't mean anything to me. The places where we lived in Baranowicze, one of them was dilapidated and rebuilt, and it didn't look the same. The old place where we lived during the labor camp in Dworec that was burned down, was not rebuilt. It's just a pile of rubbish, and I had trouble finding the place, getting myself oriented. I thought it was seven houses further down.

Now I'm beginning to figure out who, what, and when, and I located the house that I think is where our house used to be, and I knocked on the door. A lady answered and I said, "Did you always live here?" She said, "No." She said, "Who are you?" I tell her. She says, "I don't know who you are." I said, "Who lived in this house before you did?" She said, "Well, there was another house, and it disappeared, and the people's name was Maisel." I'd forgotten about that name, but when she said, "Maisel," it rang a bell. I said, "That's the place. Describe Maisel to me." She described her. She was a seamstress. I said, "Who lived across the street?" She described the people across the street with the neighborly jealousies. Maisel and this lady were both seamstresses. I hear the whole story. This lady is very nice.

Street in Dworec, 1994

Now I know I've got the right person, and we're discussing old times, and I said to her, "Can I look in the back of your yard?" She said, "No." I said, "What have you got in the back of your yard?" She said, "Why do you want to look in the back of the yard?" I said, "I used to live here at one time." She says, "You know, a funny thing happened. About 50 years ago, a boy came to my door, asked me for a shovel, and for permission to dig in the back of my yard. And I gave it to him. He goes right to the back of my yard. He starts digging and digs up all these good things. He doesn't say, 'Thank you.' He doesn't do anything, and he goes away." The lady said, "Now, we talk about it, how the boy did me wrong. But I wasn't curious."

I'm translating all this to my wife, Joscelyn, because she and my son John were with me. Joscelyn says, "She's telling your story." That's the story of how I went back after the war and dug up my daddy's gold.

We also went out to see the grave outside of Dworec. Apparently there were two graves, not one, on each side of that particular road, two and a half miles from town in a ravine. We found one of them, a marker put up by the local township. It just has four or five Russian words. Basically it says, "Victims of Nazi aggression," and that's it—no date, not the fact that it is a mass grave. There was a little fenced off area, but the fence was already dilapidated. The marker still stands. Whether that's my parents' grave, or not, I don't know. I was always under the impression that it was on the left side of the road. The marker that we found was on the right side of the road. Across the road I looked and looked for the other grave, and I never did find it. People in the vicinity that I asked never even heard of it, so you had to find somebody who was way up in age to remember it.

Mass grave marker outside Dworec, 1994

I've discussed a question of whether I should put up a marker or monument with some rabbinical sources. None of them would give me a straight answer, which they never do, as to whether I should go back and put up a monument or not. They said the best monument you could put up is among the living. The dead are dead. Basically that's the answer that I've gotten.

Outside Dworec, I went looking for my bridge, the one I built with the other boys of the ghetto. I didn't find it. My bridge was no longer standing. With the annual icing and flowing of the creek, the bridge disappeared.

I looked for the well. I've always thought the story was that after my brother was shot, he was dumped into this well. But apparently that was not the right story. The well is still there functioning, and there are no bodies in it. Never mind that for 50 years I thought that that was my brother's burial place.

I was not able to locate any of our hideouts in the woods. However, I was able to find a sample of what a hideout looked like. It is now a storage space for potatoes, and basically you can tell there is the entry underground.

I looked for the towers. The towers are now all gone. They fell apart. I found one man who remembered that there used to be towers and he showed me the tower that he thought it was. What's left of the tower are several rotted boards with rusty nails laying on the ground and, in the middle where the tower was built, is a concrete marker that the Polish engineers dug into the ground. My knowledge of geography tells me that that was not the tower that I was looking for. But the tower he showed me may have been the second one or the third one.

I was afraid to be there. I didn't see fit to research the towers any further.

I never did find cousin Shlomo's grave.

Then I went to visit my Uncle Benny's hometown, my father's birthplace, Dereczyn. Everything in there has disappeared. I could tell by the street paving where the mill used to be. It's empty space—there's nothing on it. It's overgrown. The large mill stones were standing vertically, not on top of each other. They'd fallen because the mill was no longer operative.

Mill in Dereczyn

Mill in Dereczyn, with John Winestone

Cemetery marker, 1994, Dereczyn. Ted and villager who remembered Ted's family

In my father's town, Dereczyn, I tried to orient myself, and just couldn't do it. I couldn't figure out where I was in that small town, and finally I thought maybe if I asked where the churches were, then I could try to locate things. And the church that I was asking about didn't exist anymore. But they directed me to the Catholic Church, and I walked in the churchyard, and even in 1990 it was still scary to walk in and ask for directions.

I went to see the Bliss Farm, my grandmother's home outside Dereczyn. At one time I thought it was truly a palace. It wasn't. There was some little, old house sitting out there. I asked the lady there for permission to go in. She said, "What do you want? You come to reclaim your property?" I said, "No, no. I don't want anything." She said, "There ain't no need for you to go in here." Police were sitting parked right outside; they said, "If she doesn't want you to see it, then there's nothing you can do about it."

I went to visit my hometown, Baranowicze. My hometown, where I was born and raised, was burned by the Germans when they retreated. Now the streets have been renamed. The town has been rebuilt in the same diagram, a little different. When the car dropped us off at a corner, and the driver said, "This is your hometown." I said, "I don't know which way to go." Nothing was familiar, I mean, not one thing. In fact, there used to be a statue on one side of the street. It was moved on the other side of the street, so that really confuses you. And it took me six hours to find out where I was.

After I figured out where I was, I started locating things. Everything is little. The neighborhood that we lived in is now a slum. Maybe it's a nice neighborhood now, but to us it looks a slum. There used to be a long, long, three-block walk from our house to school. It's just like around the corner now. My G-d, I mean, how could they have squeezed all these things in? There was a sawmill in between, and then there was this one's house and that one's store. There was a ditch—nothing. It's all disappeared. The football field behind our house is truly a slum. Scary as all hell.

I was only able to find all that because the way the street is paved. When I saw an asphalt tiled street, I jumped out of my car, and I asked people, "Are all the streets in this town paved that way?" Why? That was the only street in our town that was ever paved, and it was paved in the Polish manner, the old, 19th century way. So that's how I finally got myself oriented.

Of course, our home did not survive, but my uncle's house, the rich uncle's house, survived—it was burned but was since rebuilt. As I was beginning to get oriented, I was telling my son how to locate things, just to play a game, to see if my memory was all right. I said, "You go see if that building has a rounded vestibule," you know, in the French manner. Sure enough it had it, and then we asked for permission to walk in. My uncle's house is now an office building. I said, "John, you walk in and you'll see a great, big hallway." He said, "Daddy, it's not a big hallway." I said, "Are there four rooms on the right and three rooms on the left?" He said, "That's true." What I thought was a great, big, long hallway in which we used to play football, now you come in and it's just a hallway. And I said, "Now, you go at the end of the hallway and you'll find a communication center." So John goes back, and sure enough, he says, "There is no communication center, but there's a great, big hole in the wall." In other words, what equipment there was has been removed.

My hometown was a disappointment to me. No one knew anything. I went to look for the Jewish cemetery. Nobody in town knew where it was. Finally we located some Jewish graves, and it was not the Jewish cemetery. A few Jewish people lived in the town after the war, and when they died, that's where they were buried. It was just a few graves and the markers were dated 1960, 1970. That's not what I was looking for. The town had a big Jewish population and there should be mass graves where I supposed most of my friends would be buried. Gone, nobody knew where. Russians are cold blooded about it. That's a sentiment that bears no paying attention to. Some people from Israel came, and they bought a plat of ground in the city, and they fenced it off, and they put up a marker on it, "This is in memory of," in fact, it says in English, too. Had to climb the fence because nobody knew who had the key to get in. It's a forgotten issue.

·   It was a tough trip. My hometown is not my hometown anymore.

Joscelyn and I and John went back to the areas where my family went in the summers. She said, "What kind of resort is this?" It was not as big, not as fancy. It did seem familiar, but strange because it was no longer a resort, just houses in the woods. We went to look at the beach and I said, "Oh my G-d, this is the place that I was learning how to swim?!"

To go back again, uh-uh, I don't recommend it. There was no one you could talk to. There was no mayor, or no city government, nothing. I mean, it's a lawless country, a lot of people in town just sitting around doing nothing. Some old lady said she remembered my mother but maybe she did, maybe she didn't. Who knows?

Was I glad I made the trip? Yes. Glad I took my boy with me. I don't know how much he got out of it, because I made another mistake that most traveling people like this do. I started exercising my knowledge of Russian, which I hadn't spoken in 50 years, and suddenly instead of speaking to John and telling him things, I'm speaking to my driver. I spent most of my time talking to my driver.

How we ever ended up in Belarus is a miracle, and how we got out of there is a miracle. What can I tell you? It's not a place to go to. The Jewish experience in that part of the world, it was supposed to have been the culture center of Jewish learning, but it's all gone. Nothing's left of it, and the population doesn't know it. I think in Minsk I saw a sign, and the best I could figure out that they were advertising a museum about life in the Minsk ghetto. If that's what it was then at least I admire them for that, but other than that, it's a dream. It's a memory. It's a bad memory. It's gone, finished, forgotten. We've got to look to the future only. The past is gone, and that is my interview.

37. Afterthoughts: 1996, Memphis: how we did it, I don't know

The last 30 days in the woods was the worst. The first 30 days was the worst and the last 30 days was the worst.

For me every day was a struggle. Shlomo did better in the woods because he was more preoccupied with revenge for his mother's death. I tried not to talk about it, but this was on his mind constantly.

The end of the partisan story is not good. We were supposed to come back into our towns as heroes. We came back as bums. The army quickly drafted every able-bodied man into the service and left whatever. Just a few women and children were left behind. A few other strays. Then, you have to come out, and you come into your hometown and people don't know you anymore. Said, where were you? Should've been killed. In the meantime, someone else is living in your house. They got resentment against you. It's a lot of problems.

My personal opinion of the partisan effort is not that great. There were times when the group led by Atlas attacked their hometown, killed all the Germans, and maintained in town the partisan government for three weeks. Of course, the Germans came back. It was pointless. There was no reason for it other than self-gratification. What effort, what contribution that had towards the war effort, I don't know, I'm not here to judge. The only thing is that because of the partisans, I'm here, and if it weren't for them, I would've perished like the rest of them had.

The Jews had a great deal to contribute to the partisan effort. It was already started by Jews. It was later taken over by the Russians. I would say they were then 50 percent of the partisans. In Russia the partisans are considered folk heroes. The very reason why Belarus is now a republic—there was never a nation as Belarus—that was Stalin's way of thanking that particular section of Russia for their big partisan effort. The streets have partisan names. There's monuments all over. It's a big national history, the partisan movement in Belarus. However, not a word is being mentioned about the Jewish effort, now. Not one story about the likes of Bielski or Atlas or the early partisan movement.

★　　★　　★

My friends who were in the woods with me, they all tell different stories, but they're basically like mine, maybe not as colorful. Some have lapses of memory. I have a rabbi friend in Hartford, Connecticut, a former Communist. He's more dramatic. He tells the stories with greater gore, but I think I've told mine with enough description.

Friends from woods and refugee camp. Top row: Willie Moll, Ruth Lazowski, Rochelle Moll, Toby Rabinovitch. Bottom row: Ted Winestone, Phillip Lazowski

★　　★　　★

It was tough. It was heartbreaking. I don't think a normal human being could've survived it. How we did it, I don't know, we just did. There's this guy that wrote that he believes that G-d was looking after him, especially. There's a Hebrew word for it, "special attention," means "being looked after, personal." I can't say I don't believe in it. In fact, this morning when I picked up the mail at the office, there was a thank you note from a little boy. He said, "My grandfather was saved by a hideout that was built by your father." Well, what else can I tell you?

I certainly had nothing to do with it; it just worked out that way. Whether it worked out that way by design or by accident, I don't know.

This boy that I visited in Israel, Chaim Weinstein, the one who was the lackey for those two girls and their mother in the woods, now in his 80s he tells the story that he was at the original tower that I saw when I first got to the woods. He lived there for a year and the Germans finally came and attacked it. The people out there were strictly nebbishes. You'd have to be out of your mind to live in there, but they had no place else to go. And the Germans wiped them out. They wiped them out. They didn't wipe those out who survived not because they were heroic figures. It was just destined to be that way.

There were no heroes. If it was destined for you to be, so you were. And if it wasn't destined, there were people got killed the last day before liberation. There was one crazy man, a huge giant of a man, just got out of our hiding and he says he was tired of being cramped and he was going to go and he ran into a stray German. One German captured him and took him back to camp and they decapitated him. That's on the last two days of the war. How a man survives two years in the woods and doesn't make it to—I don't know.

★　　★　　★

My father's people were not day-to-day lovey-dovey, but when the calling came they stood up and they were counted, both surviving brothers were like that. I spent my partisan years, my woods years, with one of my daddy's least desirable brothers, Uncle Benny. He was forceful in a different direction, real odd person, loud mouth. But he did the best he could, and really it was through his activity that I survived. Uncle Benny took me in, in the woods. Although I was treated miserably, I was still with him. And Uncle Herman: We weren't the greatest of friends, even to his death, but when the times were rough and your contribution meant something he stood up, a lot of people didn't. So I'm proud of Uncle Benny and Uncle Herman.

Uncle Herman Weinstein

My Uncle Benny in later years used to claim that he saved my life.

Ted and his uncle Benny (Benjamin Weinstein) about 1986

What's true is that with persistence and luck and guidance by Feldman and Robinovich, he kept himself, Florence, Marvin and me alive. He was just lucky that way.

For 40 years, whatever travails and problems my uncle thought he had, Uncle Benny only knew in his mind that had he stuck with Feldman in America, everything would've been alright, and would I please find out where Feldman is, and he'll go see him. And then I got that call from Uncle Benny one day. Uncle Benny never called me really. I said, "Why're you calling me?" (I always called him). He says, "Feldman died." And, that's when I knew it was the end of an era. Now, it may sound comical only because I make it so, but one man's prejudice and one man's superstition you know, <laughs> maybe is a lifesaver. Who knows? I don't know. I'm not here to analyze.

★   ★   ★

My son, David, is named after my daddy, and my daughter, Rebecca, is named after my mother. My daughter Shelby is named after my brother Noach Zelig. Joscelyn and I named our son John after my cousin Shlomo and my uncle Jona. We named our daughter Izzy (Marie Isley) after my uncle Israel Iskiwitz and my mother-in-law Marie. I couldn't name any of my kids after Great Aunt Tillie (in Brooklyn, my grandmother's sister) because my first wife's name was also Tillie, so I could not honor my aunt as I wished.

Aunt Tillie was a very religious person, and she used to drop casual hints about not becoming irreligious. And out of deference to her, and other reasons, after I got married I became religious. Prior to that it didn't make me any difference, so maybe that answers a question that you wanted to ask. My Aunt Tillie is the source of my religious behavior. You've got to set an example for your children. You've got to tell them who they are, what they are. I hope I have done that.

Epilogue

After Ted has recounted what he lived through, listeners often ask, so what happened after the war? After you came to America ... then what?

After the war, Ted, age 17 in 1947, finally gained approval for and made passage to America where he settled with his mother's sister Tillie in Queens, New York. Completing high school within a very short time, he went on to work part-time while he attended classes at City College of New York. When his Aunt Tillie suddenly died, Ted took the train to Memphis and settled in with Israel and Dora Iskiwitz (Israel had previously been married to another of Ted's aunts who had been killed in Poland). With the loving support and guidance of his uncle and aunt, Ted earned his bachelor's degree at Memphis State University (now The University of Memphis). Subsequently drafted, he served for two years in the U.S. Marine Corps during the Korean War, attaining while on active duty the rank of Staff Sergeant. Proudly Ted became a citizen of the United States as he fulfilled his military obligation. As a civilian he returned to Memphis, took a job as an accountant, passed his CPA exam, and went on to attend night school through which he earned his Doctor of Jurisprudence degree.

Each survivor's story is unique; each survivor's journey is an individual one, fueled by the experience and emotion of that person. Ted's path has been a demanding one, but has been lightened by his prevailing sense of gratitude. Whether this sense of appreciation was a deliberate choice he made or whether he was blessed by this gift is a mystery beyond our intellectual limits. But it has indeed led to a life that spread before him with grace. Gratitude allowed Ted to marry and have three children, to survive divorce and remarry, having two more children. Gratitude filled his heart and overflowed to the many people he has helped along the way, with material and emotional support. Ted has enabled many degrees to be earned, funded many small businesses that have led to livelihoods, and even assisted people wishing to become U.S. citizens. He has made a way for others' dreams to come to be. Hopefully all of these individuals inspired by Ted will likewise help others.

In the Jewish community, Ted is a staunch and reliable supporter. He helped establish and has supported the Memphis Hebrew Academy, finding enormous pleasure in providing the means and opportunity for all of his children and grandchildren to receive a Jewish education. This story could be one story—a child's world, maimed by inconceivable cruelty. A child's heart, irreparably torn. But this story is another one. Not shying away from the brutality he suffered, Ted pulled himself towards a life of achievement and happiness, acknowledging each person that encouraged him, helped him, loved him. His words are invaluable, because they trace a life that resisted the atrocities that almost ended his life, that did end the lives of most of his family. His story is a vigorous affirmation of life, a resounding "yes" in the face of hatred's blight. This story will be read by his children, and grandchildren, and great-grandchildren. But it is a story that should be read by all who want to reach a knowledge of our origins and our journeys and how to live with grace, with gratitude.

—JW & TM

Editor's note

When I was approached to help preserve Ted Winestone's remarkable story in a book, my first task was determining my role. Would I serve the story best as writer, editor, interviewer, ghostwriter, something else? To start, I watched several long interviews that Ted did for the Shoah Foundation, and then I read the full transcripts of those interviews and interviews he'd done with Tara McAdams. I knew almost immediately that my work would be to shape Ted's words for readers, not to retell the story in another voice. These interviews contained the full story, and Ted's storytelling was masterful—moving, suspenseful, full of telling detail, unexpectedly funny—and distinctively his own.

To grasp the whole picture, I began putting the stories into chronological order. I was still open to other ways of organizing them at first but the further I got, the more I saw that this order really worked. It made it much easier to understand how everyone was related—that seemingly infinite number of cousins and other characters who would stroll into the story at key moments—and just how many family members Ted lost in the war. Most of them and the other main characters now appear in the opening sections when Ted describes his background and early life; when they come back onstage later, as the reader will see, I inserted brief explanatory phrases.

Determining the chronology was not always a straightforward task. Rather than presenting one big story, Ted told many smaller stories. Responding to questions as much as to his own memories, he jumped around in time. Different interviewers elicited slightly different angles on the same events. In one interview he might go straight from A to B, and next interview he would tell an entirely new story that included unsuspected but essential events between

A and B—impressive storytelling, and a fascinating challenge for his editor. Most difficult for my chronological imperative, internal details didn't always clarify the sequence. Quite understandably, the time when he got very sick in the woods is almost out of time altogether, a nightmare inside a nightmare.

My third big decision, after determining to center Ted's voice and order his account chronologically, was to delete repetition. Talking and listening are very different from writing and reading, and to make Ted's voice accessible on the page I ironically had to trim a lot of his words. At the sentence level, I took out repeated turns of phrase that he used to set rhythms or fill time while he was thinking, though I retained enough to sound like Ted. To win structural clarity, I reluctantly sacrificed an important dynamic: Ted told, retold, and circled back to the details of some of the most emotional stories—the end of the labor camp, the German soldiers walking over his group's hiding place in the woods. While very moving to the ear, on the page this dynamic did not serve the larger story. I was honestly startled when, the editing done, the story of his worst days in the woods ran just a few pages. (Readers can still watch the interviews and read the raw transcripts.) I also worked to preserve how Ted often speaks in a way that echoes how he learned to live in the woods—getting by with just enough. Here, that careful economy is also more than enough to convey the intensity of his experiences.

My largest editorial challenge was where to place the terrible story of what happened to Ted's parents. The events occurred in the 1940s, but he did not learn the full story until decades later. I tried it in both chronological places and finally discerned that the organizing principle of the overall story was not only chronology, or when things happened, but also biography, or when things happened to Ted. So the revelation is towards the end of the book, where the reader can also see how it helped form Ted's reckoning with the trauma of his youth.

Ted and Joscelyn Winestone graciously fielded a lot of questions about very difficult experiences. When I could not figure out something or was unsure of any particular editorial move, I left a query on the page for them. Robert Gordon and Tara McAdams brought fresh eyes and great questions to the new text. This book has been a collaborative project, always in service to Ted's voice and Ted's story.

I am honored to help bring Ted's story to a new audience. He resisted fear and terror with courage, and transcended hopelessness and grief with generosity and determination. May his account of both the fragility and the resilience of humanity help us forge a better future.

Laura Helper
Memphis, 2019

Author's Bio

Ted Winestone was fifteen years old when he emerged from two years of hiding in the Polish woods, surviving World War II. He came to America in 1951 and served in the Marines, became a CPA in 1956 and an attorney in 1960. He lives in Memphis, Tennessee.

CPSIA information can be obtained
at www.ICGtesting.com
Printed in the USA
LVHW091212210420
653475LV00004B/2